Pioneering Women Speak

Transformative Leadership on The Rise

Curated by
Winsome Duncan

Published By

2021

You are strong &
beautiful
Grow your colours.
J-Carter

PEACHES

PUBLICATIONS

Published in London by Peaches Publications, 2021.
www.peachespublications.co.uk

British Library Cataloguing in Publication Data: A catalogue record for this book is available from the British Library.

ISBN: 9781838147235.

Book cover design: Peaches Publications.

Editor: Winsome Duncan.

Typesetter: Winsome Duncan.

Proof-reader: Joanna Oliver.

Table of Contents _Toc83549154

Dedication

Pioneering Women Speak is dedicated to the bold and courageous women of the world, who continue to champion change, mainstage and behind the scenes. Always remember your authentic power within and share your gifts on a global scale.

Acknowledgements

Each of the women who have contributed to this book remain thankful for the creativity in our hands, the talents bestowed upon us to be Leaders in our own lives and therefore enable us to inspire renovation in others.

We intend to acknowledge the Change Agent in you and pay homage to all women; past, present and future. We thank our ancestors, who have guided our path, whispering wisdom to fuel our intuition as we travel on the winding road of life. We fit into different places and spaces around the globe yet come with a unique message of optimism and motivation. Giving a voice back to the voiceless, we rise. Wombman, be not afraid of situations you cannot control, find peace and comfort in letting go.

Today, give yourself the gift of learning and growing, through the wisdom of the women present within these pages. We aim to engage and acknowledge your sacredness by paying it forward, to enable future generations of women and girls to not only elevate but to become their own Visionary Pioneers.

We salute every single girl who has matured and now resides on Grown Women Avenue. Today, we see you and adorn you with a precious investment in leadership, vision, transformation and progress.

Arise Warrior Queen

Pioneering women speak
at the crest of dawn,
in tongues of ancient wisdom.
Robed in the secrets of a wise sage,
given to the ages in Kente cloth.

Her crown
is coiled in the silver of her hair
and her need to care.
Even in dizzying heights of fear,
she dresses well for the occasion.

Practicing patience
underneath her fragile wings, that glide
over mountain tops, in anticipation.
No, she will never stop,
wrapped in purpose, passion and pain,
with eyes that glisten like gold.
She is on a mission to rediscover her whole soul.

As she grows gracefully in the wind,
she knows tomorrow is never promised
to the expectant.
We commune and chatter around campfires,
manifesting our deepest desires.

Spiralling ever-higher,
vibrating through the midnight wire.
Praying for insights to set alight our dreams.
And when we 'fall apart at the seams',
I am my sista's keeper and together we soar,
transforming with eyes that sparkle and gleam.
Standing firm together on tomorrow's dream.
While we scream, when rediscovering voices lost in
our childhood wilderness.
The healing forest is thick
with promise of regeneration, to pour forth into a
nation, with bated breath, we hold hands at the
mending fence.

Stepping forth and birthing all nations.
Becoming the ultimate healing creation.
Wombman, take your stand and mount the shoulders
of injustice.

Taking responsibility for her swelling pride and ego,
that bathed her in protection and guarded her
secrets till death,
while they whispered in the wind.

May we begin to dance our blues into florescent
orange sunsets,
that smell sweetly of forgot-me-nots.
A muse of her time, born to win.
Creating a better reality
is simply her designed destiny.

While the world sleeps,
her heart beats
to the circadian rhythm of sweet mother earth.
She wakes up the sheeple
hypnotized by foreign lands,
whilst holding the epicentre in her hands.
Her placenta providing the nourishment for aching
sores, she looks up and walks away from closed
doors.
Arise great warrior Queen,
for together the mighty must stand.
Arise pioneering women and make your demands!

Winsome 'Lyrical Healer' Duncan.

Introduction

In this Anthology, you will explore the mental tapestry of nine dynamic female entrepreneurs, who seek to make the world a more inviting space.

The reality for women in business enterprise and development can often be a lonely place. These diverse authentic stories of unity are worth reflecting on and celebrating, for the women who tell them not only survived, they are still standing strong.
With a keen focus on equality and inclusion and embracing our differences, we are able to create some unique content.

70% of the authors are neurodivergent and are also new to book writing. *Pioneering Women Speak* will encourage you to consider your tenacity, as you immerse yourself in the powerful stories of dreams deferred, courage, resilience and creativity spilling from the pen. The overriding theme is *Transformative Leadership on the Rise* and our wish is for you to continue to support and help us to implement these potent messages, globally.

London-born Writer and Number One Bestselling Author, Winsome Duncan, is the CEO of Peaches Publications. She is an author of sixteen books and a Book Confidence Coach, renowned within the publishing industry.

The Anthology, *Pioneering Women Speaks* is her pilot collaborative project, which started with a compulsion to make publishing affordable for busy entrepreneurs, who were time-poor. Her vision was to enable inspirational women to work collectively and build a legacy which would be documented in the British Library. The authors had to complete an application and were carefully handpicked to contribute to this momentous project. Lived experiences are embodied via shared insights around the topic of business, self-development and spirituality.

In 2020, amid the crisis of the global pandemic, people and businesses found themselves adapting to a 'new normal' and emotional stresses were faced by most of society. Winsome curated a collective think-tank, to explore and reflect on lessons learned, some of which is reflected in the anthology you hold in your hands. We continue to chant and champion all of our aspiring and established authors; join us on this amazing maze of truths and big reveals.

The chapter titled, *Love Letter to my Younger Self* is fortified with textured wisdom of the ages. We want the reader to identify and learn from 'shoulda, woulda, coulda' of life-long hurts.

Make sure you keep a journal close by and use the reflection notes at the end of each chapter, as an opportunity to develop your personal growth. Located at the back of the book are the author biographies, should you wish to continue the journey and connect with them on social media.

The Pioneering Women Speakers are:
- Winsome Duncan
- Marcia Brissett-Bailey
- Melanie Folkes-Mayers
- Shona Kamau
- Joanna Oliver
- Ruth Pearson
- Anna B Sexton
- Patricia Bidi
- Linnette James

Unity and a collective consciousness are required when challenging the old system and ways of doing things. Together, we can make an impact and change the way in which women show up in the world of business. We advocate for all female voices to be heard and traverse the sea of corporates that often choose to keep us muted. This is takeover season and we are ready, not only to sit at the table, to also pick up our knives and forks and to eat.

Patricia Bidi and Winsome Duncan

Winsome Duncan
Book Confidence Coach

www.bookconfidencecoach.com

www.peachespublications.co.uk

"The body stays at rest until a greater force moves it."

Newton Laws

Reflecting on Resilience

Definition - Resilience: *noun*
1. one.
    the capacity to recover quickly from difficulties; toughness.

Source: www.dictionary.com/

Peace be still! For it is only inside the solitude of your mind, shall peace ignite the tranquillity for your soul to be still. Great ideas are birthed in quiet spaces. We need to breathe more deeply and exhale the stressful toxins of this life journey. We are living in a condensed world, with a takeaway generation mindset, wanting daily instant gratification on a plate. Oh Lord, please hear my cry, for in the wilderness I fear my shadow. Nothing is sacred anymore; house doors are no longer left opened. We are just expected to gloss it over, put some rouge on it, be strong and continue on.

"Hands up, don't shoot", has become the Black Man's anthem and the women who love him stand back incapacitated. I cannot breathe, take your knee off of his neck, are scenarios that are seen globally, yet where is the love? Are we supposed to pick ourselves up regardless of the tel-lie-vision that lock us in mind-prisons? This leads us to self-medicate and numb ourselves to out-of-key frequencies. We 'change the station' to the fact that the world is in crisis. I cannot have my breakdown, no not today, please wait, my emotions are still loading. When chaos is in your home and envelops you, my message today is, 'peace be still'.

The dictionary says that the word 'resilience' is a noun and its definition is, 'the capacity to recover quickly from difficulties' and, 'toughness'. Let us break this down. This chapter is called *Reflecting on Resilience* because I truly believe that in order to get anywhere in life, there comes a point where we stop being everything to everyone. This is especially true when the silver hairs start showing and you look in the mirror at the wrinkles when your eyes smile and you recognise time is no longer your friend, you become aware to the time-wasters in life. There comes a day when we must sit down and reflect on where we have been, where we are right now and where exactly we plan to go. This is not a luxury just for the visionaries, this is a tool for everyday people who want to improve their lives and do extraordinary things. This should be a self-cleaning kit for all humankind; to process and ponder.

During the pandemic, we had the opportunity to break from our habitual rat-race mundane lives. Most of us had at least 18-months to exhale and press the reset switch. Even if we still worked during this crisis, there was still an atmospheric reconfiguration taking place globally. We had nearly two years to think about, what is it that we really want from our lives? Are we living on purpose or on a wing and a prayer? Did you spend your time wisely or was it squandered away on Netflix?

Getting back to the case of resilience; the word 'capacity', is the first part of the definition. What do you currently have the capacity for in life? What is brimming in your cup that overflows and cannot stop? What are the messages that you are not listening to that are permeating your existence? Sometimes we are so busy and exhausted that we are running away from ourselves. Have you ever stopped to ask why?

Disingenuous people can give us the illusion that they are 'all-knowing', yet there are cracks in their lives; they just hide their dysfunction better. How can one preach healing, when they are sick? How can one teach wealth principles, when they are broke and are living from pay-cheque-to-pay-cheque? How can one teach health and still binge eat on cakes? How can one be an alcoholic and tell others not to drink for their own safety? Sounds contradictory to me. The fake facades only fade when we become willing to address what ails us. Then we wait till our circuits are overloaded and a myriad of heart attacks and strokes are on their way to teach us the lessons that we thought we knew but were just 'fronting'. Today, brothers and sisters, I need for you to look at your capacity boiling point, with a new lens and break down the barriers.

Your intuition speaks to you all the time; however, are you listening? Intuition is the spirit of discernment. Are you paying attention, or are you just choosing to ignore that quiet, still inner voice? Are you making the choice to continue to be that factory raggy doll that must be all things to all people, at all times? Are you wiping yourself out with addictions, workaholism, alcohol, drugs, gambling or sex? Are you pretending that you are okay, however on the inside you are burning up because you feel that it is never going to be okay? When does your mask slip? I hope you have conceded that currently, we are in serious times.

When we talk about capacity, how much do you have left to hold onto? How much more can your heart carry before it breaks? An Interesting fact is that the majority of heart attacks happen first thing Monday morning, when people are getting ready to go to that job, that they hate and see that Manager that they just want to slap in the face. See, I have been there and done that and became a whole heap of unhappiness, chiselled inside of depression, on my best day. I have lived that experience countless times and rebelled, however there are no more blue Mondays for me. There are:
- Busy Mondays
- Creative Mondays
- Stressed Mondays
- Money Mondays
- Day off Mondays
- Admin Mondays

Like Robin A. Sheerer champions, there are definitively 'No More Blue Mondays' for me, now that I have found my purpose in my creativity. I understood that I have the capacity in this world to show up artistically. When we are looking at the word, 'resilience' and the definition for 'capacity', I am asking you today to state, what is your personal capacity?

Let us move on to the next part of this resilience definition, 'to recover quickly'. That almost sounds like an oxymoron to me, to 'recover quickly'. The thing about resilience is, in life society tells us that we must have nerves of steel and still wear that 'everything is fine' smile. It does not matter what's going on, let us just 'skin some teeth' (smile) and everything is going to be alright. However, sometimes it is not all right, it can be all leftfield or you are just slap-bang stagnant, in the middle. Sometimes, recovery means staying in your bed and not wanting to go out and live life. Sometimes, it is suicidal tendencies and you wanting to get out of your thoughts. At times, you are spiritually bankrupt and you want to give up. You cannot cope with the children, the husband, the wife or your tedious day. You cannot handle the crazy-makers in your life. You have just enough in the tank to hold on by your fingernails. The rent is due; the money is diminished and you are in your overdraft. You are in deficit. You are a minus, so who will deposit into you now? When a cheque bounces, it is because of insufficient funds; what insufficiencies are you dealing with today? Where are you emotionally deficient? What are we recovering quickly from; the bruises and the traumas of life? Are we recovering from the mental stress of the last 18 months of pantomime pandemonium?

Can we really force a speedy recovery? The Mary J Blige documentary, 'My Life' comes to mind; the fact that she did not smile and had to fight all of her life. It gets weary sometimes to realise that you're in your 50s and not your 40s or even 30s; time you will never get back. Now do you see the relevance of where I am taking you in this chapter? Time is the most precious commodity you have and you must use it to heal, rest and restore.

I hear alarm bells ringing when the dictionary says to recover quickly because sometimes, my people just need respite. Sometimes, we just need to rejuvenate. Sometimes, we just need to breathe, to exhale. Let go and let God. If I am to be resilient, I have to recover quickly and bounce back. Sometimes there is no elasticity in my bounce-back muscles anymore and what then, how do I recover quickly? Do you recover quickly by pasting on that happy smile and some lipstick, or splashing on some aftershave? Yes, I am alright, however I have just had a minor stroke. Yes, I am fine, however I am just working through my migraine and blurred vision. Oh, I am good, however the blood vessel in my eyes have just burst and the Doctor said I should rest; however, I will be okay. As a regular sufferer of migraines, I know that this is my body telling me I am doing too much; get some rest, stay off the computer screens and go relax.

God will throw a pebble, then God will throw a rock. If you are hard-headed and do not listen, God is going to throw a boulder in your life. The dictionary definition says to 'recover quickly'; however why, why, why do we have to recover quickly? Why is that embodied in the definition of resilience? Why can we not be resilient and take a break? I want you to look in your life to determine, where are you having to recover quickly? What are you recovering quickly from? Are you even healed yet? Are you healed from the trauma of the past, the present and to come; because if you are not, you are just going to continue to bleed out. You are going to haemorrhage on the star-studded stage, called life. When we are talking about resilience, where is your self-care? Where is your, "let me take a break, it is breathing time" moment? Where is your exhale switch? Where is your self-love? Do you have a time-out card?

Okay, then the final part of this sentence is from 'difficulties and toughness'. In life, there are times when you need someone and there is no one around. You are all by yourself. Ain't nobody coming to save you anytime soon. Now, I am talking from a place of being in solitude for much of my life. I like to just do my own thing; however, it is not necessarily healthy to isolate. Difficulties in my life caused me not to be inter-dependent. I was a one-woman show. I can do it. I'm gonna do it. I AM doing it. All I was doing was just covering up the greatness of who I am and hiding my authentic self. Why? Because it was easier that way? Why? Because it was more comfortable to sit in my mediocrity and complain and do nothing about the issues that were going on in my personal life, in my work, my relationships and my finances? It was easier for me to sit in that comfort zone of mediocrity, rather than face the toughness and the difficulties of the dramas that were going on and presenting themselves in my life.

There are going to be many difficulties for some of you, maybe most of you that are reading this book; however, it is how you bounce back that really counts. How you recover in the end, is what really matters. You need to acknowledge that life is a roller coaster and it is going to go up and down, left and right, in and out. You need a plan of action related to how you are going to adapt. How are you going to stand? How are you going to function through those challenges? There is a Bible scripture that I really like and it gives me strength. It gives me peace of mind and it comforts me. Whenever I read it, I feel like I am on track. It is from Ephesians 6:13, (NIVUK)

> *Therefore, put on the full armour of God, so that when the day of evil comes, you may be able to stand your ground, and after you have done everything, to stand.*

That is my second message to you today, STAND! My personal experience of reflecting on resilience means to simply firm, stand shaky, stand wobbly; however, stand. Stand on your dreams. Stand on your hopes. Stand on your aspirations. Stand on your vision. Stand on the dreams that God has poured and buried deep inside your soul. Stand on the intuitive voice that tells you to take a breather. Stand on the creative abilities that flow through you, know who you are and know whose you are, in the struggle. You have to get up, stand up and be counted. We need to hear your story today. I do not know what you came for, however I am telling you now, reflecting on resilience is a way to get up and be acknowledged. Cry those tough tears. When crying season lands at your doorstep, let those tears fall, to water the flowers of your life they can bloom.

My personal definition of resilience is of a person who understands self-actualization and has the ability to adapt to any situation that is presented to them, with a perspective that the cup of life is half-full. No matter what they face, they will stand up on their two feet, to that experience. Back to tough tears, in troubling times; when crying season lands at your doorstep, let those tears fall in the midst of your adversity. What do I mean? Sometimes, you just have to cry long, cry hard and have a really good cry because crying releases endorphins. You know when you have that feeling after a cry, you feel so much better, right? You feel amazing, sometimes. You can feel like, "I can move mountains now". I know that sometimes tears can be sad and feelings of anxiousness take over and you might not feel strong enough to cry, however, understand that feeling your emotions is a perfectly natural thing to do. It is a perfectly fine way to exist in this world.

So, when you go through seasons of grief with a profound loss, a breakup of a relationship or a friendship, let the tears fall where they may land, in the midst of your challenge or your adversity. This is quite crucial because it is okay not to be okay and let no one tell you differently. Take off your superwoman and superman capes and stop running around. Stop and smell the flowers and feel the grass between your toes. It is not about a candy-floss-coated idealism; let's pretend, let's do it all in one or a happy-clappy dance with rainbow dreams. That is not the goal. Go to a deeper level, knowing and exploring the warmth of your soul experience. It is about the realism of who you are and unearthing your best life yet. Once those tears have dried, the next step is for you to become still. I opened this chapter with 'peace be still'. Did you know that in stillness, dreams are birthed? Did you know that in stillness, you can hear the call of God over your life? Did you know that in stillness, your intuition rises? Inside stillness, there is peace that surpasses all understanding! Hush! Be quiet, be silent. Shhhhhhh! Do not speak, close your mouth, button your lips. Just simply sit in the awesome power of who you are; it is vitally important.

If you are going through something, know that it shall come to pass, like an ocean wave washes over your soul. We have different seasons of life. We have seasons of nature, winter, spring, summer and autumn. Life will rotate on the earth's axis. The reason why some people think about suicide and take their own lives is because they do not see any other option; they feel there is no other way out. All they want to do is stop the feelings; however, we always have choices. I want to breathe life into your deferred dreams, through this text. As short as it may be, I want you to feel lifted, so that you can go forth and be your best authentic self. You can go forth and spark your healing revolution. Be bold and empowered, so that you can be inspired on any given day of the week. In the words of the late, great Edgar Guest, "rest if you must, however, do not quit".

You can be like a strong tower inside resilience and you can rest assured that when you are ready to come back, the return of your spirit will simply be to stand firm on solid ground. As you prepare to read the other stories of powerful female energy, in this book, know that there is a couple hundreds of years' wisdom collectively speaking to your spirit.

Life and death are on the tongue. You can cast spells over your life, or you can speak life into your dreams. I hope you have enjoyed this chapter, reflecting on resilience, through my lens. There is so much more to say, we have only just begun. Do check out my

reflection questions and take the time to make some notes at the back of the book. Just begin to know that everything is alright as it is and you too shall recover. When you know better, you grow better!
Peace.

Reflection Zone

1. When you fall short in life, how can you maintain balance?

2. Why are your tears a sign of strength?

3. Create three disciplines to redefine your perspective on resilience.

4. Write down your three core strengths.

5. Write down three areas for emotional development.

6. What are your three blockages to creating time for reflection?

7. How, in your view, does resilience mean you are weak or strong?

8. What are the three new ways you are going to show up in this world?

9. What does 'authentic resilience' mean to you?

10. How can you stand firm with clarity, when moving forward?

Marcia Brissett-Bailey

Neurodivergent Consultant
SEND Specialist and Career Advisor

LinkedIn ID: Marcia Brissett-Bailey

"If you're always trying to be normal you will never know how amazing you can be."

Maya Angelou

Embracing Neurodiversity in Business

Understanding Creative Emergence

I am dyslexic, with my own unique fingerprint and it would be wrong of me to state that every person with dyslexia is creative. I can only talk from my own journey and lived experiences regarding the neurodiverse advantages dyslexia gives me, through a creative medium.

My creativity is extremely personal to me, based on cultural differences, individuality and how I view the world from my unique standpoint. Therefore, it is extremely hard to compare one person's creativity with others.

I see words in pictures and pictures in words and I have always found this magical, creating my own little world, where I create big visions. As a child, daydreaming was very natural for me enabling me to block out the external world. Hours felt like days and days felt like years, however, it was only a moment in time, of my personal and internal thoughts. Escapism would feed my mind, to create with intention and that is when the magic would happen.

It has taken time for me to really find my voice in the world of words; to discover the self I've wanted to become since my early childhood aspirations. This has required that I continue to evolve and build, with skills such as determination, passion and hard work. I've had to navigate and hack my way through an educational system that did not include or represent me. Just because I approached the world from a slightly different lens, I frequently felt like I did not fit in or belong.

If only I was able to see and understand, what I see and know now; I wonder if it would have given me a different path of opportunities. I know I have a disruptive approach and enthusiastic way of thinking, in business. This is especially true when I have a keen interest in anything I do. I am organised, good with dates and pay attention to details. I never feel like I am working when doing something interesting and time just slips away. This may appear as a different type of normal to some but a linear approach can be sometimes crippling for me because it stifles my growth. However, I understand linearity has its place. I discovered that thinking differently has some advantages, as well as creating synergy in order to connect the dots. Alongside all that I have mentioned, social aspects, such as feeling valued and safe, can play an integral part in how one performs.

I have always had an artistic mind and used my imagination to create pictures through storytelling and I have always liked to draw, which enabled me to escape from the real world. I had the ability then and now, to visualise a project and see the bigger picture, seeing the end goal before the beginning. I do this when I am in the kitchen cooking, whilst creating new dishes in my head and seeing the ingredients all in my head. However, over time I have come to realise not everyone can see in pictures.

All of my ideas would float around my head, yet I just could not put my thoughts into words on paper and found this excruciatingly frustrating. What I have learnt from these feelings of frustration, is the importance of being kind to myself and being able to look in the mirror and say, "I love me" with meaning. It is so important that you love yourself, especially when there has been trauma in your life. A good place to start on your journey, is knowing yourself in the following areas:

- Self-identity
- Self-awareness
- Social protocols
- Self-confidence
- Self-esteem
- Self-management

These concepts have helped me to understand and manage my emotions to self-motivate and have positive interactions in all aspects of my life. It all starts with knowing who I am at a grassroots level. I show up to be counted in life on a daily basis and this is a ripple effect, which spreads across my family unit. I have had many conversations with my inner voice, providing myself with positive affirmations and soft prayers to God/creator. I needed to adapt in finding ways to achieve my goals and with hope, I was always able to see light at the end of the tunnel. I also learned to see failure almost like an illusion, as no one ever really fails at anything; everything we do produces a result. All those efforts to read and write, and my past teachers 'red pen' remarks, highlighting mistakes in my work or areas of improvement, tells me now, that I never failed. I simply produced a result that did not match my peers and/or hit prescribed school targets. There is so much judgement based around 'standardised' testing, which has nothing to do with intelligence, that we develop fear of making perceived 'mistakes'. With current accepted 'norms' and strategies, how does one grow and develop?

I have asked the question in my mind many times when I have been tested on my memory or assessed on my written work. Is knowledge more important than creativity and imagination? I see beyond a blank canvas; curiosity, willingness to take a risk, persistence, passion, resilience, empathy and unconventional thinking, are all qualities that enable me to see value and full potential all around me.

I think about my ten-year-old self, who struggled to understand the world that was presented to her. Now years later, in my adulthood, I am no longer ashamed to say I have a form of word blindness and language-based barriers. I have learnt the, 'feel the fear and do it anyway' approach to life. I embrace my Neurodiversity and now know it is good for business.

We all need to embrace the parts of us that make us authentically unique, countering the need to fit in.

Youth Leaders of Today

Many parents (myself included) are always looking for ways to expand our children's minds, especially when it comes to entrepreneurship. My husband being an entrepreneur and property investor and us being parents to two children, we are keen for our children to have opportunities to develop a creative and investment-centred mindset, with the intention to create a road map for them to find their 'why'.

It is widely accepted that planting entrepreneurial seeds early on in the fertile soil of young minds, can be highly rewarding. For example, I would wake up at 5 a.m. every Wednesday morning with our daughter to help prepare for her pitch stand, which was a business start-up project during her primary school years. This was an initiative to help children understand business and she would sell fresh apple and ginger juice and make cinnamon popcorn. This became very popular at school, especially with the teachers (!) and was her first lesson in supply and demand.

From this, she learned about income, outgoing expenses and profit margins. It also taught her about work ethics, understanding finance, leadership, working hard, being committed, instilling consistency, accountability, communication and interpersonal skills, alongside project and time management. Since then, at the end of Year 6 in Primary School, she has created her own business, 'Yani Creations'. This showcases positive affirmation through images of nature. She wanted to motivate her peers who were finding their exams stressful, helping them to turn negative thinking into positive thoughts.

Your young person may have dreams of becoming a footballer and may not see the future in business. However, taking on a business approach, does not do any harm. We live in a technological age, advancing in areas of automation, which is diminishing the idea of the traditional 'job-for-life'. Now more than ever, it is important to recognise we have moved towards an ideas-based economy.

We have understood that the foundation of encouraging children to think laterally can be as simple as a walk in the park and exploring nature, being curious and having fun on the way, whilst creating an inquiry-based mind, questioning the way the world operates. Taking advantage of activities in your local area is a good cost-effective move. As an example, we have taken the children to activities at our local library, which included Astronomy and Chess club. Creating a parents' network is also an effective way of encouraging parents to share information about developments at school, clubs they attend, or events in our local area. This can also encourage children to develop their network of like-minded peers.

We have always allowed our children to draw their ideas on paper, exposing them to creative thinking and finding their voice by expression and emotions. This could be imagery, poems or a quote and we believe creative thinking is a necessity to write their own content and be their own destiny. All creativity starts with an idea.

Being exposed to these concepts and ideas during their most studious years, means the deeply ingrained knowledge will likely continue throughout their lives. Empowering our young people with golden nuggets of wisdom includes for us the African proverb, 'it takes a village to raise a child' and the 'Go alone, go fast, go together, go far' mindset. My husband and I very much believe in this philosophy, which is strongly embedded in us from our Caribbean cultural upbringing, meaning the entire community of people in our network, including elders, family and friends, all have a role in the upbringing of our children, with our guidance. This interaction, we believe, plays a significant role in enabling children and young people to experience and grow in a safe and healthy environment.

For example, our children attend a mentoring programme where they get support from the community of people, to build their connection and tribe. We feel this raises children's self-esteem, self-worth, confidence, identity and can create a sense of belonging. A supported community usually has a vested interest in empowering and passing on knowledge, to raise a young person's aspirations and follow their own personal dreams instead of living vicariously through us.

Making mistakes (and being okay with it) is such an important part of growing up, especially if working towards being an athlete or an entrepreneur.
It is so important that children and young people have the opportunity to enjoy the things they do and to not worry about doing them perfectly, all the time. We believe that letting go, moving on and trying again, are all mantras of successful entrepreneurs.

It is imperative in business management that if something in life does not go to plan, you have a back-up plan, as well as the ability to pick yourself up and try again, looking at the problem from a different angle or perspective in order to move on. One attitude I see our children have, is adaptability and being team players, due to engagement in all their sporting activities over the years.

Education, especially primary education in my experience, lacks connection to the modern world. Assistive technologies can support some children to access learning and technology in a different way, as they may learn differently. I feel our current infrastructure is outdated and there needs to be more cross-working partnership initiatives. Working to a standardised test does not develop creative or soft skills. We should no longer be preparing young people within an industrial framework, as we are not preparing factory workers. Contemporary society requires growth mindsets; it is about building content, creative branding or taking a 'disruptive' approach to improve an existing foundational entity, for example. However, many of our schools are trailing miles behind where they need to be, in order to support children in the 21st century.

We do not consider ourselves to be experts on parenting, however in reading our experience, you may reflect on the opportunities that may more effectively help to cultivate aspirations in our young people. I believe being creative enables our children to make connections between one area of learning and another, which will further extend their understanding and 'connect the dots'. This includes art, music, dance, role-play and imaginative play; nurturing appreciation of the importance of creativity and the role of education in encouraging creative development.

Being a youth leader today is not always about business, it is also about having fun and making connections, creating space in for them to use their imagination and opportunities to just play. Being creative itself produces knowledge that may not otherwise be discovered. I believe that being an entrepreneurial parent is about building a foundation and providing the stepping-stones that enable our children to reach for their fullest potential and goals.

Goal setting
All life forms have a natural urge to move forward, adapting to survive and thrive, unless there are environmental factors or barriers hindering this. It is our intrinsic purpose, to work towards a goal; as people, especially children, grow and develop and move through their life cycle. New aspects of life will emerge, which could take us off course, due to the impact it has on our whole life. This is when we need some motivation and possibly some guidance or support along the way.

Setting a goal helps us to identify what we want to achieve and is the first step towards translating intention into action. An action plan identifies what steps are needed to get to a destination, by breaking it down into achievable chunks.

As a qualified career advisor and working in guidance for many years, supporting young people and adults, I have developed a personal development programme on goal setting, for students who are neurodivergent. I have a toolkit of resources and strategies for goal setting and holding ourselves accountable in realising capabilities that we never believed possible. In doing so, we can push a person to achieve, with the intention to transform mindset. This is the approach I generally take in my own life. I also take risks by first assessing the challenge, accepting it, then undertake the learning and 'bumps in the road' along the way. There needs to be a desire for change and movement and an element of drive.

This chapter would not have happened, if I did not invest the time and set a framework of short, medium, and long-term goals, in order to achieve the end goal of completing this chapter. It is a process and with any goal there may be obstacles but if you prepare yourself for the reality of life and circumstances, then you are better able to be flexible.

In the final part of my chapter, I would like to share some practical tips to help you visualise; setting goals with key points, which is an element of my toolkit in supporting others to make informed choices.

The SMART action plan toolkit:
Specific:
- What are you going to do?
- How are you going to do it?
- Where are you going to do it?
- With whom are you going to do it?

Measurable
- Making your goal specific, means it should be easy to measure whether or not you achieve the goal.

Achievable
- Set goals that are realistic and within reach. There is nothing wrong with dreaming big,

there just need to be some stepping-stones and strategies around the goal.

A note to self: as I have mentioned earlier in this chapter, failure is an illusion. I pose the question - are we ever failing, if we are trying? We may need to look at our goals from a different perspective and accept this feedback. It may not always feel easy and you may sometimes need to feel physically, mentally and emotionally ready, in order to move forward in the process. This comes from my own experience of setting personal goals.

Relevant
- Do you think the goal is relevant to you? It is important you can see a clear link between your goal and how this will impact the aspects of your social and emotional, health and wellbeing that are important to you.

Timely
- Is the goal the right thing for you to achieve right now?
- If yes, set a time frame in which the goal can be achieved.
- Perhaps consider setting mini goals, so that you take smalls steps to achieving bigger ambitions.

Explore Importance, Confidence and Barriers
- Self-confidence building may be required - use a scaling system to measure.

- People are most likely to successfully undertake the action and achieve their goal if their confidence is 7 (out of 10), or greater.
- Explore the barriers and identify steps to work around or change these.

Some examples of questions to help make a SMART plan

- "What specifically, would you like to be different?"
- "What specifically, could you do to get started?"
- "If the first step is successful, then what?"
- "Who else could you ask for support, if anyone? What could you ask for?"
- "What might get in the way of this plan? How could you overcome these?"
- "What would be the signs that things are going well?"
- "How would you know when you are off-track?"
- "What would you do if you were off-track?"

Before you set any goals on your journey to creating your possibilities, you need to have an open mind to the opportunity and the right mental attitude for achieving your goal. Nothing on earth can change or move forward if you do not have motivation and a positive mindset.

Goal setting is a tried, tested and popular method for achieving, in any area of life. I had a vision and set a goal to become an author during the first lockdown; my intentions were clear and it has been a process to learn, grow, ask questions and seek support in order to achieve my goal.

Reflection Zone:

1. What does being creative mean to you?

2. How can you adopt creativity into your daily life?

3. What skills can you work on together, in your family/household?

4. How can you create daily goals for yourself, to achieve positive outcomes?

5. Set three goals that you can achieve by the end of the year, (remember to keep them as SMART goals).

6. What are your child's strengths? What steps could you put in place to enhance your children's learning?

7. What have you learnt about yourself when working with others, are you aware of your strengths?

8. What are some of your most powerful learning moments and what made them so?

9. When do you feel most creative and what do you do about it?

10. Name three activities you could do, to be more entrepreneurial.

11. What is your inner voice telling you to do next?

Melanie Folkes-Mayers

Human Resources Specialist

www.edenmayers.com

"If you do not like where you are, move. You aren't a tree."

Jim Rohn

The Keys to Effective Recruiting

The Science of Hiring

We all reach a stage in our businesses, when we realise that we need additional support and skilled expertise to be able to take our business to the next level. However, handing over elements of our business baby to someone else can be extremely difficult. You need to be confident that you are recruiting the right people, with the right skills, at the right time.

1. Are you super nervous about hiring staff for your business?
2. Do you want to build a team but do not know where to start?
3. Have you hired friends or family members to assist you in your business, only to end up regretting it?

If you answered 'yes' to the questions above, then, this chapter is for you.

I meet with potential clients who are exhausted and shattered by trying to do and be ALL THINGS TO EVERYBODY. Conversely, are those who have a small team of staff, yet feel like they are more trouble than they are worth! Both eventually take a huge toll on us and our mental wellbeing.

It does not have to be that way.

With the appropriate preparation and framework in place, you will be able to build a team that will support you, as you scale your legacy-building business.

Michelle's Case Study

My client, Michelle, is a super busy new mum who needed to recruit an Operations Manager; someone who could be her second in command. This would give her the time to focus her energy on growing her website design business, whilst being secure in the knowledge that all of her existing clients are being taken care of.

Michelle was not new to hiring staff, as she had a technical team of five. However, she had struggled to find an experienced Operations Manager and had previously recruited two others who did not have the skills that she expected and were unable to project manage and motivate her remotely based team. She felt stuck; she knew she would not be able to take on additional clients until this vital role was filled, with a qualified person for the job.

Using my signature, 'Hiring For Growth' system and tailored-made processes, we were able to identify the ideal candidates for her business, advertising the role in the correct places and shortlisting to a strict criterion. I carried out the first round of initial interviews and then Michelle and two key members of her team carried out the final interviews and selection exercises, with the three top candidates. It took just four weeks to secure Michelle's ideal candidate, freeing her up to build her business and spend quality time with her husband and daughter.

This scenario is also possible for you and you can have a thriving business and fulfilling life. There are three key elements to recruiting effectively:

- Establishing Your Organisational Culture
- Knowing what you need
- Recruiting the right person

Each component is essential to attracting the right employees, with the right skillset, at the right time.

As a leader, your role is to empower your team to develop and deliver their best, so that they are fulfilled in their job. Next, I will take you through the foundational steps of my hiring system.

Establishing your Organisational Culture
Before you start building your team, it is important to have clarity about your organisational culture, as it will help you to define your ideal team members.

The first step to defining your organisational culture is to establish your businesses:
- Mission
- Vision
- Values

I like to describe **Mission** and **Vision** as your businesses **Departure** and **Arrival** destinations. Your mission is what your business does, for example, my Eden Mayers consultancy's mission is:

To provide tailored, expert Human Resource skills that a client needs. To confidently manage, motivate and develop your team so that you can focus on building and scaling your business for growth.

This is what my clients receive from my business in each and every interaction with us. Please note that business mission statements very rarely change and remain the core foundation of your company.

When writing or reviewing your business Mission statement, a good exercise is to go back to focussing upon your 'why':

1. Why did you start your business?
2. What need is your business fulfilling?
3. What is the reason your clients come to you, as opposed to another company?

Having a company **Vision** reflects where you decided you want your business to be in the marketplace. Eden Mayers' is:

"To be the go-to HR company for Small to Medium Enterprises (SME) in the United Kingdom, with at least sixty percent of the market share by 2021."

Your Vision should be easy to articulate. You can choose to create your one, three, five or ten-year aspirations with your staff. It's important that you can visualise the path and share your company objectives with your team, as you take them on a growth and development journey. You do not need to have all the answers (no one ever does), however you do need to know what your success-markers are and how you can achieve them.

You need to be able to clearly articulate your Mission and Vision to your candidates and team members. They should be the golden thread that links business, team and individual objectives, which I will discuss further in this chapter.

Your **Company Values** should be linked to your business Mission and Vision and should be three to five keywords or phrases that you can use to describe the way that you do business. For example, an Active Wear clothing retailer may have sustainability, innovation and health as their core values. This should mean that they are not a fast-fashion brand and that their clothing is designed to enhance their customer's athletic ability and confidence.

The important thing is to have values that you can demonstrate; it is pointless having "sustainability" as a value if you do not recycle, reuse or reduce your consumption, as this is not in line with your company values. These values need to be experienced by everyone who interacts with your business.

If you are currently running your business as a solopreneur, a good exercise is to ask ten people how they would describe your business in three words; ask those closest to you and throw in a few clients too. You will find some similarities, so it may even surprise you.

If you already have a team, ask them for suggestions. You could narrow it down to the top ten and then ask them to vote and use the top three as indicators of how your company is perceived externally.

Once you have decided what your values are, use them in a paragraph to describe your business, Eden Mayers HR are:

*We are **Dedicated** and **Focused** on helping businesses and individuals progress positively.*

*We are **Knowledgeable** about our business, experts in all areas of HR, data analysis and project management.*

*We are **Efficient**; we can work quickly and help you get the results you need.*

Putting your values into a paragraph makes it easier to share with potential team members and ensure that there is no ambiguity in your expectations.

Knowing What You Need

Often as business owners, we know that we have too much work and need some assistance. However, we may not have a full understanding of what is needed to give us the free time that we require to rest, restore and replenish.

When I worked corporately, I had a remote HR admin team, that was located in Somerset and because the process of in-person training was made more complex, I tended to do things myself. I processed redundancy calculations for 100s of staff; however, by the third time, I was wondering why I had not invested the time in training them. I was spending a huge amount of time on administrative tasks, which was not a good use of my time or skills. Have you ever had a similar experience?

I have worked with business owners who insist on doing the credit-control chase ups themselves because they believe that no one else will do it as well as them. Then they proceed to complain that they have an administration resource but they still do not have time to focus on growing their business. You must strive to work *on* your business, as much as you work *in* your business.

The main aim of building a team is to free up your schedule. This way, you can deliver within your Zone of Genius, as championed by Gay Hendricks; the expertise that you are uniquely qualified to deliver and to create the systems that have the most positive effect on your bottom line. That could be strategic planning, making a product or delivering a service. It could also be networking, speaking engagements and creating new products or services. My Zone of Genius is problem solving; I get to the heart of an HR problem and find the best tailored solutions for my clients. It is pointless to build your team if you are unwilling to let go of the reins and empower your team members to work within *their* Zone of Genius.

You must ensure you hire the correct person with the acumen you require. Start by identifying all the tasks that happen in your business. I tell my clients to spend two weeks collating a list of each individual role they carry out, even down to mailing and shipping. Be really thorough with this list. Once completed, create a table and separate the essential tasks that you need to deliver personally and the tasks that could be automated or outsourced.

Bonus Tip
There are many systems that can support you in automating your business processes, for example 'Asana' for assigning tasks and project management, 'Acuity' for diary management (including setting up zoom rooms), 'Xerox' for sending recurring invoices and so forth.

Once you have done this, you can start to build your role(s). When I did this for my business, I realised that I needed administration to help with client accounts, diary management support, marketing support and a HR advisor. This did not mean hiring three full-time employees, it meant building my team in a manner that was sustainable for my business functions.

I started by finding a Virtual Assistant (VA) who could carry out my marketing activities and automate my invoicing and diary bookings, by utilising software and systems.

Once I had my VA and automated processes in place, I was able to review my tasks again and create the job description and person specification for my HR Apprentice.

So now you know how to work out what you need, let's help you find the perfect consultant, contractor or employee.

Recruiting the Right Person
Did you know that 33% of new consultants, contractors or employees leave their jobs within 90 days? In 'Psychology Today', Stybel Larry (2019) highlighted the top two reasons for employees choosing to leave, which were:
- The role did not match their expectations
- The organisational culture of the company was not in line with their values
- The role was too intense

Whether a new team member leaves or has their contract terminated, it is a loss to your business, incurring wasted time and expense, interviewing, inducting and training. In reality, three months is generally the time frame when an employee can work to their full potential.

The average hire will cost you approximately £4,000, more if you use a recruitment agency, so it is vital to ensure you hire the best person, the first time. The key document for your recruitment process is your Job Description and Person Specification, which should attract your ideal candidate and repel all the others. The advert you create, interview questions and selection exercises should all come from elements of your Job Description.

Your Job Description should begin with an OVERVIEW OF YOUR BUSINESS; when it was established, what the role is and why the role has been created. You should be able to take a lot of this information from the Mission, Vision and Values statement that you created in the first section of this chapter. You want your ideal candidate to read those first two to three paragraphs and think, 'I want to work here'. The next section should give detail of the role, including:

Job Title
Make sure that you call the role something that your candidate will look for, for example, 'Head of

Happiness' is not the standard job title for an HR Manager and wouldn't be searched for on Google.

Main Responsibilities
A paragraph detailing the key responsibilities of the job role.

Reporting
Clarify the line of management the role will report to.

Direct Reports
Will the successful candidate have team members to manage?

Location
Where will their main place of work be? Remote, London or New York?

Contract Type
State the contract type as permanent, fixed-term, ad-hoc, zero hours, full-time, part-time, term-time and so forth.

<u>Salary and Hourly Rates</u>
Dependent on the contract type, you could give a salary, project-based or an hourly rate range. Be sure to research the average salary for your role, to ensure that you are offering a competitive rate for the role.

The next section is the interesting part; this is where you outline the MAIN DUTIES of the role. The thing to remember is that you want to highlight responsibilities in paragraphs, rather than creating a list of tasks, for example, if you have 'Marketing' as a section and write:

1. Write engaging content
2. Post to Facebook
3. Post to Instagram
4. Edit and upload videos to YouTube

What happens when you decide to try finding your ideal clients on TikTok, Clubhouse or LinkedIn? A better option would be: *To create, curate and post engaging content across our social media platforms, daily.*

The next and final section is the Person Specification, here you want to list the essential and desirable skills, also known as what I am prepared to teach or train and what I am not. Remember the more essential skills the higher the salary or hourly rate is likely to be. The personal specification is generally divided into the following categories:

Qualifications

What qualifications are essential for the role? GCSEs in English and Maths, Accounting Qualification, a degree in Software Engineering?

Relevant Experience

What work experience would make them an ideal fit for your role? For example, six months' experience of working in a customer-facing role, one-year marketing agency experience, two years of team management experience?

Aptitude, Skills and Abilities

This is a really big element, where you detail the systems-knowledge and software skills that you are looking for, such as, Microsoft Office, Canva, iOS, Adobe suite and so forth. You would also detail soft skills, like attention to detail, clear communication, time management and the ability to prioritise.

Once you have your Job Description and Person Specification complete, you can start advertising your role.

Are you Attracting the Right Candidate?

When it comes to attracting your ideal candidate, you have to remember that this is a relationship-building exercise, not very different from the relationship that you establish with your clients.

Treat your candidates and team members like your ideal clients. You need to understand their drivers, pain points and desires. Is your ideal candidate someone looking to move up to the next level in their career? Or are they a parent who wants flexible work around their home responsibilities? Are they passionate about working in their community or are they motivated by money and influence? Your job advert needs to speak to their desires, they need to read it and think, "I am perfect for this job".

Knowing the type of candidate will also help you to advertise in the right places; it could be your local college, on LinkedIn, through your network and/or using job boards.

Using my signature Hiring System, I have helped clients in the UK, Europe, Australia, Canada and the USA recruit locally and internationally, dependent on their need for consultants, contractors and employees.

Having a detailed job description and person specification makes it easy to attract and select your ideal candidate.

I recommend that you ask candidates to apply with their CV and a cover letter, stating how they match your job description as a minimum. Dependent on the role, you may also ask them to submit a portfolio, respond to a case study or research something too.

I have candidates, now what?
Once the applications start rolling in, you will need to screen your applicants; I use a matrix, with all of the criteria from the job description and person specification and score them according to their CV and supporting documents.

Once that is completed, I recommend that you telephone the top ten and ask them a maximum of five questions to ascertain their interest in the role and key skills and score this to decide on the top three candidates that will be interviewed.

I suggest that alongside interviewing your candidates, you have at least one selection exercise too, such as a presentation, a social media concept or case study.

You want to get a feel for how they work and how they will work with you, your team and your clients. Just like a telephone interview, create an interview matrix to ensure that you are asking all candidates the same questions and scoring accordingly.

Try not to interview alone; if you already have a team, get one or two members of your team to join you. If you do not have a team, ask a friend to sit in with you so that you have someone to discuss the candidates with. Now you have found your ideal team member, it is time to make a killer offer!

*Remember to give feedback to all of the applicants who took the time to apply to the job role and let them know that they have not been successful. No one likes to feel that their application just disappeared into a black hole. Also, just because they were not right for this role, does not mean that they will not be right for another one at a later date.

Preparation is the key to effective recruiting. Follow the steps in this chapter and you will be building a team of brilliant go-getters in no time.

Reflection Zone:

What is the Mission of your business?

What is the Vision for your business?

How are you going to achieve your Vision for your business?

What is your Zone of Genius? (The thing that you are uniquely qualified to do).

What tasks in your business would you like to hand over?

What is holding you back from starting or building your team?

If money were not an issue, what would your ideal team look like?

What are the characteristics of your ideal employee avatar?

Where do you want your business to be in five years' time?

How will you feel when you achieve your business Vision?

Shona Kamau

Christian Life Coach

www.virtuouslivingbygrace.com

"The decisions you made yesterday affect your today. The decisions you make today affect your tomorrow."

Deanne Williams

Faith in Business: No Compromise

Faith and Doubt

I had a lot of emotions inside of me, when starting my business and becoming a Christian Life Coach. I was excited, joyful, determined, hopeful, felt optimistic about what my future held and empowered. Finally, I am walking in my God-given purpose and ministry, supporting women to heal and find self-love and acceptance, after emotional trauma. This work gave me a sense of fulfilment in building my business; having an inner sense of peace.

I need to know myself and stand in the authority of God, when it comes to my business. I need to lead by example, which requires me to have a good sense of direction and that direction can only come from God, being that it is a God-ordained business. Being able to trust God with all my heart and lean not on my own understanding but acknowledge Him and He shall direct my path. Acquiring knowledge and wisdom from the source in order to then have discernment in my business. I can then truly lead a faith-led company by not compromising on that faith. One example relates to situations where I should know when to and when not to speak, to then give God all the glory in my actions, especially when I keep calm after receiving negative feedback on social media. I have had a couple of people saying awful things which have been quiet upsetting. I have had to learn to have discernment, wisdom and to be wary of who I take advice from online and in person.

I am proud of my Christian ministry and often find comfort in God's biblical word. Even though we may not be of the same faith, I want you to hear the essence of how I found the courage to transform my life from dark times. Moving into the next chapter of my life as a young woman, is where I experienced challenges within my faith.

Faith, what is Faith? Well, God says faith, as it is written in Hebrews 11:1 - The Passion Translation (TPT):
"Now faith brings our hopes into reality and becomes the foundations needed to acquire the things we longed for. It is all the evidence required to prove what is still unseen".

Hebrews 11:3 - The Passion Translation (TPT):
"Faith empowers us to see that the universe was created and beautifully coordinated by the power of God's words, he spoke, and the invisible realm gave birth to all that is seen".

As it is written in Psalms 46:10 – New King James Version (NKJV):
"Be still, and know that I am God".

2 Corinthians 5:7 – New King James Version (NKJV), states:

"For we walk by faith and not by sight"

Hebrews 11:6 - The Passion Translation (TPT):

"And without faith living within us it would be impossible to please God. For we come to God in faith knowing that he is real and that he rewards the faith of those who passionately seek him".

Did I act in faith? Or did I act from a place of doubt in the beginning of starting my business? I acted from a place of doubt, I could not see the vision God had for me clearly, so I sat and did nothing with my talents. *Was this displeasing to God?* Yes, because I did not trust His process. I was trying to compromise and do what I felt comfortable in the earthly realm. However, God spoke to my spirit time and time again; have faith and do not compromise. A scripture that often comforted me was Jeremiah 29:11 – Amplified Bible (AMP):

"For I know the plans and thoughts that I have for you,' says the LORD, 'plans for peace and well-being and not for disaster, to give you a future and a hope'.".

Let us find out *what does God say about doubt in business?* Philippines 4:6-9 - The Passion Translation (TPT):

"Don't be pulled in different directions or worried about a thing. Be saturated in prayer throughout each day, offering your faith-filled requests before

God with overflowing gratitude. Tell him every detail of your life, then God's wonderful peace that transcends human understanding, will guard your heart and mind through Jesus Christ. Keep your thoughts continually fixed on all that is authentic and real, honourable and admirable, beautiful and respectful, pure and holy, merciful and kind. And fasten your thoughts on every glorious work of God, praising him always. Put into practice the example of all that you have heard from me or seen in my life and the God of peace will be with you in all things".

Wow, how powerful is that? I also experienced a lot of doubtful moments in my career, if I am honest with you. I was continually anxious and I had so much negative self-talk. I felt like, 'God, I cannot do this, I feel so ill equipped. My truth cannot help no one, who am I? You cannot use me. I am not good enough. I am not whole enough. I do not even know where to start. No one is going to listen to me. I will not be heard. I am not a celebrity. What I say will not bear any weight; use someone else. I am just not good enough for this purpose. Why me, Father?'

If, you know the Lord, you know all of those words spoken, He had something to say to counteract each and every one of those doubtful moments in my life. My God is so powerful and merciful. He took me on a lesson on how to endure spiritual warfare. I go into depth with this in my second book, *Loving Yourself God's Way*. God comforted me and helped me understand I was a new creation in Christ. The Devil does not want to see me win, so he planted seeds of doubt in my mind which grew into negative self-affirmation. However, God said I must not lose sight of the end goal and he is saying it to you too. We must guard our mind, body and soul, which is pleasing to our Heavenly Father in our businesses and other areas of our lives, so He can rejoice and be glad.

It is so natural for us to have self-doubt, in setting up our business because it is new; something we have never done before. It is uncomfortable stepping out of our comfort zone, as we all like to be comfortable, right? But if God has given us a vision and told us about our purpose, who are we to not walk in that purpose and trust God's guidance? So, what did I do and what can *you* do, to make the transition smoother?

Our faith can increase by feeding ourselves even more with God's word, put on the full armour of God every day, as a form of protection. It is how I enter the world to help cover me from negative forces. Take every thought captive to the obedience of God. Do not compromise on who God says we are and what we are capable of doing in our lives. We are exceptional beings because He has given us a purpose and that purpose needs to be fulfilled.

Self-awareness in Christ
In business, it is always good to have a spirit of discernment. The dictionary defines self-awareness

as, "knowledge and awareness of your own personality or character."

However, self-awareness in Christ is the ability to be able to keep a close watch on yourself and on the teachings of Christ, by examining yourself to see whether you are in the faith and walking within the fruit of the spirit, which are godly characteristics. With God's divine power, He is then able to grant us all things that pertain to life and godliness, through His knowledge, not our own.

Taking up our heavenly Father's cross in our daily lives and following him, we can start finding our true identity in Christ, as we sacrifice ourselves to find our true selves within our heavenly Father's eyes.

As it is written in 1 Timothy 4:16: Easy English Bible Translation:
"Think carefully about how you live and about the message you teach, continue to teach God's true message, then God will save not only you but also those people who listen to you."

As a Christian Life Coach in my ministry, I am being used as vessel like it states in Philippines 4:6. - The Passion Translation (TPT):
"Don't be pulled in different directions or worried about a thing. Be saturated in prayer throughout each day, offering your faith-filled requests before God with overflowing gratitude. Tell him every detail of your life".

It is not about being pulled in different directions as a Leader or Director of my company, Virtuous Living by Grace.

If I did not have the self-awareness that comes with knowing who I am in Christ, I would not be able to lead by example. I could have made wrong decisions which would have led me in a direction which certainly would not have brought glory to God, in a business He has ordained to help women.

I used God-given discernment, wisdom and prayer when I met naysayers and wished them well. This portrayed a godly characteristic, which was then pleasing in God's eyes and did not compromise my faith in order to please others.

Having self-awareness in Christ, in your business, means fully understanding and writing down your mission, your vision, your why, your purpose, your strengths, your goals, your weaknesses and being able to make the correct choices. Do not be emotionally-led in your business, especially if it is not growing as fast as you would want it to; I speak from experience. Sometimes we want to rush the process but during the process, there are things we need to learn along the way. We need to be so self-aware, knowing our personality, our godly characteristics, by having faith and waiting upon the Lord. As it is written in Habakkuk 2:2-3 – Holman Christian Standard Bible (HCSB):
"Write down this vision; clearly inscribe it on tablets so one may easily read it. For the vision is yet for the

appointed time; it testifies about the end and will not lie. Though it delays, wait for it, since it will certainly come and not be late".

Honouring God within Business
When starting out in my business, I never stepped out in faith. I was more uncertain, not knowing if I will be accepted or knowing if I would be heard. I never believed in my talents or the insights God has given me.

However, God made it very clear to me that my story of trauma and what I went through, the lessons I learned along the way, the gifts He had put in my hands was not mine alone. I should not sit on these, as they needed to be shared globally. So many women would be impacted and break free from the guilt and shame of the past. I should be a light to the world because the products that I offer and the services I provide, are needed in this changing world. God advised me that my business is instrumental and would glorify Him and bring people to His Kingdom.

I should always remember that He is number one over the business and **I should converse with him daily about my duties**. He has given me the gifts to bless others and He produces my wealth and that should not be my main focus, as he kindly told me I should not be greedy or selfish with the wealth he would provide because:

"Those who want to get rich fall into temptation and a trap and many into foolish and harmful desires that plunge people into ruin and destruction".
1 Timothy 6:9 – New International Version (NIV)
Instead, He told me to **honour him with all my first fruits and he will make my business overflow.** So that highlighted to me even more so, that everything will not be in my will but will be according to my Father's will.

I started to give my first fruits (monetary offering) to the Lord, which **honours God by being obedient to his word, allowing him to be Lord over my life and business.** This means godly principles need to be in place, not just on the outside of my life where people see but on the inside where no one sees. I cannot honestly honour Father without doing that.
As it is written in Matthew 4:4 – English Standard Version (ESV):
"Man shall not live by bread alone, but by every word that comes from the mouth of God".
Roman 8:28 says:
"And we know that for those who love God all things work together for good, for those who are called according to his purpose".

Another way **I honour God in my business, is by making sure I always do what is right.** As a Christian Life Coach, starting out on Instagram was really hard as I started to compare myself with others, in terms of how many followers I had, how many likes I was getting, questioning whether there were enough engagements on my posts. I was always checking and making comparisons. I was always looking at the audience, how many people followed me in the last seven days, how many people unfollowed me. Sometimes, I would get disheartened thinking, 'what am I doing wrong, how many accounts have I reached in the last seven days? and yet again, I would get disheartened.

Can you relate? As that is also normal on social media, I found. However, if no one tells you, you will not know, **so** yet again instead of trusting God within the process, I allowed the enemy into my mind. I never took the thoughts captive, which is a topic I teach about in my forthcoming book, *Loving Yourself God's Way*. I tried to speed up the process instead of waiting on God's timing. I tried different loops such as getting 759 followers by following 15 people. Imagine, this is like you're cheating God, that is not allowing your followers to grow organically, that is rushing the process.

How many of these followers would actually engage with your content? Buying follows and advertising because it was quicker but the connection is not there and the engagements, well I did not see the fruits of that labour. When contributing to another loop I purposefully said this time I am going to come out of my comfort zone and start networking, engaging, having conversations, exploring where I can share my story. It was lovely doing that because I built really good connections. However, it was still not honouring God because I was still trying to skip the process. Another way which I dishonoured God in my business, was buying followers, which was dishonest in my opinion.

I saw my Instagram grow to over a thousand followers. It looked so good to the external eye, however to me God said, "Did you honestly get those followers?" Of course, I said no. "Are you truly happy with how you got them?" Again, I said no and they started to drop 10 by 10 and then he said, "Take them down". I took them down. I felt so free in doing that as I could truly get to see God at work behind the scenes. I can honestly tell you it has been amazing trusting the process. My following has grown and it been organic. I am sharing my stories of my personal alopecia journey which resonates with so many, who are then inspired to share their own stories with me. It has been absolutely amazing seeing what God can do when you fully commit. Like in Proverbs 16:3:
"Commit your works to the Lord".

Here are the seven ways I have honoured God in my business:

1. Praying over my business every day.
2. Allowing God to be Lord over my life and business.
3. Honouring God with my first fruits.
4. Honouring God by being obedient to His biblical word.
5. Honouring God by making sure I always follow the moral ethics of His teaching.
6. Honouring God by trusting He will innately direct my paths in my business.
7. Honouring God by serving the people who He has called me to serve, with a clean and pure heart.

I was then honouring God in my business and trusting He will direct my path for His perfect timing. When you invite God in with your business plans, He is able to bring the right people to you. He can use you as a vessel, by being the light, where He can use the gifts He has put in your hands. So, like me you can then help, support, encourage, inspire and motivate others around you. God has sent us to serve, for people to be able to step into their greatness.

I Interviewed a couple of inspirational women to give you more insights on how you can honour God within your business and restore balance.

Three ways that Jemma Regis, the Author of *God's Romantic Getaway,* honours God in her business:

1. **Praying over everything in business and life by** asking practical questions and expecting an answer. Now the answer may come through the word, it may come through circumstances and events, it may come from somebody speaking to me, it may come though God speaking directly to me during my quiet time. I do not move until I get the answer. My prayer has been recently, "God give me the unique concept that will enable me to stand out from the rest."

2. **Allowing God to be my spiritual business partner,** which allows my business to thrive.

3. **Honouring God by making sure I do what it is right**. My faith is important to me in business. Not wanting to get jealous or to be envious of other people or become disheartened in regard to social media. I have learned more recently to stay focused on what I am doing and every time I do that, I feel empowered because my thoughts are now focused on the direction that I am going.

Jemma Regis states, "my faith is very important to me, especially in regard to my business because my journey with intimacy with God, has taken my faith and business to another level. I also want to know that my spiritual business partner, God, is with me every step of the way, and that every move that I make, He is there guiding me and protecting me."

Afia is a born-again Christian of 19 years and the owner of Afmena Events, specializing in elegant floral and event designs.

Here are the four ways she has upheld and honoured God within her business:

1. Sunday being the Lord's Day, where I hear the word and serve the church community and choose not to work on that day.
2. Honouring God by doing what is right, by registering my company and making sure my taxes are up to date, she quotes Matthew 22:17,21 New King James Version (NKJV)
   "Tell us, therefore, what do you think? Is it lawful to pay taxes to Caesar, or not? Jesus replies."
   "... Render therefore to Caesar the things that are Caesar's and to God the things that are Gods."
3. Honouring God with my tithes, which is honourable and having integrity with my finances.
4. Honouring God by putting him first in my life and business.

Afia states, "As a result, I can hand on my heart say that my business is blessed. I have had opportunities which have completely blown my mind. A recent accomplishment was having Ian Wright as a client, when he had a welcome back party from being on, 'I am a Celebrity get me out of here'."

Reflection Zone:

1. How would you describe your attitude to taking responsibility for every area of your life?

2. Every morning, I want you to write down your inner thoughts about the world.

3. How would you describe your attitude to faith?

4. Have there been times in your life where you lost faith in something?

5. Where do you feel you have compromised in your faith?

6. In what ways do you seek God in your business?

7. Write down three ways you can protect yourself from the secular world?

8. What are the three ways you will not compromise in your business?

9. What does it mean to honour God?

10. Write down three ways you can honour God in your business?

Joanna Oliver

Personal and Professional Growth Mentor

www.consultachameleon.co.uk

"Act like you know the truth because the truth is, we REALLY do know the truth!"

Iyanla Vansant

Grow Your Colours

It has been my pleasure to help many people over the years to write their books, through mentoring, editing and proof reading, alongside harbouring a sense of having written my own books, "inside my head". The following chapter provides a glimpse of what I would identify as my forthcoming 'signature book', where I offer a 52-week ideas and growth strategy, via a collection of actions and mantras that I have found helpful along my somewhat scenic journey.

'Grow Your Colours' symbolises being and becoming who we authentically are, by expressing our full and genuine selves. It is my belief that everything we need is already within us and rather than collect strategies for achievement, I champion a holistic internal growth process. In growing our colours, we can experience from the inside, the many shades, hues and depths of who we are and be ready to fully embrace ourSELVES. Life is a journey of both process and destination and we are constantly presented with opportunities to learn more about ourselves and thus discover more of our colours.

This chapter is written from my heart centre; it is about me, it is about you, indeed it is about all of us. It is where I share how growing my own colours has enabled me to create a career trajectory that reflects who I am as a person. My professional 'toolkit' is diverse and my career definitely reflects this 'portfolio' identity. Sometimes I may be editing manuscripts, other times recording content for my 'bids n pieces' podcast, the next delivering my personal development course, 'Grow Free From Shackles', alongside raising funds for charities, writing social media content, developing organisational policies and lecturing at university. As a mother of three, with a home-educated seven-year-old, this type of bricolage career suits me, enabling me to juggle my obligations.

I refer to professional development as synonymous with personal development because they are inextricably linked, each influencing the other. I champion living in alignment and cannot, nor do I want to, separate 'work' and 'home', as 'personal' and 'professional' are dynamic, in an interplay with each other. Perhaps the professional provides a veil for us to hide behind, a way of behaving and performing not 'giving too much away' about who we really are as people. The merging of personal and professional is not without It is caveats; it can be challenging. However, on balance, it can enable us to create a lifestyle where the priorities of work and home shift focus according to what is happening in life – which, as we know can be unpredictable at the best of times, especially in this day and age!

I believe that engaging in personal development is not to highlight one's own or another's lack or need for correction. It is however, about acknowledging vulnerability and knowing that it is *okay* to be vulnerable, to be open to growth and change. If reading about the idea that you could be vulnerable is leaving you cringing and feeling uncomfortable, this chapter is *definitely* for you; keep reading.

I have read many personal development books and blogs and listened to audio books and seminars and what I have learned is that *nothing* is new, that it is the same information repurposed again and again. Yet in a universal sense, *everything* is new. Our journey, even if cyclical, is always significant. What is interesting is that different messages reach a variety of people, in a range of situations. It does not matter how far along your journey you travel, there is always need for regeneration, for some food, for some soul sustenance. So, let us feast.

The Art of Growing Your Colours:
The opposite to a colourful life cycle, is a monochrome life, governed by a prescribed set of rules, where our identity is a shadow of the 'real' person trapped inside, usually narrated by 'shoulda' and 'woulda-coulda'. It becomes problematic when we 'should' on ourselves, all day long. This life is often characterised by a measure of discontent, manifested as an inner scream and accompanied by an overbearing sense of feeling misunderstood. In this world, the secretly-sought-after-life belongs to another, trapped behind the screen of the self-imposed norms and expectations of our so-called comfort zone.

A fundamental aspect of growing your colours is in allowing yourSELF to be playful, by tuning into your 'right' brain – the side that is open to free flow and does not overthink. Creativity is key and it is important to allow yourself to play, explore and enjoy life, perceiving it as an adventure full of exciting twists and turns. Imagination is our fuel and the art of growing your colours involves acknowledging where your creativity lives, nurturing it and injecting it into your everyday life.

Being in creative flow, means that we are open and receptive; this is the space where synchronicities reside and once we start to observe these, we become aware of magical moments of manifestation! Along the way, we find our kindreds, which intensifies the creativity, with energy multiplying in capacity, as a uniquely evolving process. Many of my work-based partnerships have evolved in this way, whereby a seed is planted and nurtured with the nectar of opportunity, growing in its own sweet way to become what it was always intended to be. The beauty in this process is undeniably exciting and it is how I love to work. However, it is not for the faint-hearted! It requires a level of trust in the adage, "letting go of the outcome" and believing that, "what will be" is truly what is supposed to be.

With creativity at the heart, I have never claimed to have a blueprint or system for growing your colours. Indeed, I am diametrically opposed to this approach because following a prescription is surely the antidote to creativity. Growing your colours is art in action and the most I claim to offer is a framework, where change and flux are accommodated, where it is 'okay' to change your mind and where resetting the compass is embraced. Afterall, to remain stagnant is to die a little inside every day. Many people are fearful of change and expend energy trying to keep things the same, rather than to step into new territories. If your energy is calling you *there*, why are you *here*? In fact, it is sometimes in the discord, where we find our buried treasure; our vulnerabilities bear untold gifts, if we could only de-layer and allow ourselves to be content with not being okay today, then we have found true freedom. I remember reading, 'I'm okay, you're ok' by Thomas Anthony Harris, when I was at university.

The book was revolutionary in my journey and has marked my travels since. Having an underlying and an overriding sense of 'ok-ness' and recognising that some of the internal conflicts with ourselves and others comes from not feeling good enough, or from dealing with someone who does not feel fine, has saved me much angst over the years. It enables me to be comfortable with my vulnerabilities and to recognise their value and honesty in my life. More recently, I have read work by Byron Katie, 'Loving what is' and Brené Brown's, 'Daring Greatly: How the Courage to Be Vulnerable Transforms the Way We Live, Love, Parent, and Lead', who both promote embracing our vulnerability.

Creativity helps us to ground ourselves in the 'now', which is a powerful reminder of the transience of life. Yes, it is important to plan, however, to do so at the cost of becoming, can be stifling. When we set our focus too far ahead, on the things we want to achieve, we do not appreciate the moment that is life. We are always being guided - sometimes gently, like a cool, soft wind and at other times abruptly, with a hardy slap in the face. The more we tune in, the less the message has to hurt; perhaps this is why I am fond of the famous Caribbean saying, "If you cannot hear, you must feel".

These messages, often reflecting consistent and perhaps repetitive themes, will often reveal to us our purpose. Life is short and in varying ways, we are all seeking. Tuning into your purpose and taking action to tangibilise it in your everyday life is incredibly satisfying and contributes to a real sense of contentment and peace. We must listen, listen and listen again, even if sometimes straining our ears because even those messages that are constricted, are meant to be heard.

I often use daily quotes and popular sayings that inspire me on my journey; one of my favourites is that, "we cannot unknow what we know" and when hearing messages, we must be clear that they are responses to innermost questions that we harbour. Thus, it is important to follow the guidance we are sent. Asking the question and then not waiting to hear, or *wanting* to hear the answer, is unproductive. It is important to be open to hearing the response to the questions we seek and to follow the guidance. If we are attuned, we will know deep down, if what we are doing is what we are being guided towards and is our 'soul' purpose. In my view, this is an ongoing act of mindful connectedness with others and our environment and it is very easy to become out of synch. Regular honest reflection, quiet time, prayer and meditation can help to counteract this and helps us to join the dots. However, we need to be proactive in our self-care and not pay homage to lip service.

'Everything is everything', as Lauryn Hill referenced in her song; see the bigger picture in Technicolor. Dream in colour and in rhyme, join your own dots for self-preservation of your own skills and talents and also the dots across your life. The connections between you and others and across your various activities and acknowledge the synchronicity, in how everything can feed each other.

I love the saying, "everything happens for a reason". In a very simplistic way, it reminds us that although we may feel we are in control, we are not, and this is what makes life the adventure that it is. Appointments get cancelled; trains are late; there is traffic on the road. However, the notion that everything happens for a reason, means that we can relax inside the laws of synchronicity, let go and just accept what has happened. We cannot change it and therein lies the art of letting go, to go with the flow and enable this to propel us forward. Go with the art of growing your colours!

The art of growing our colours is crucially about acceptance and don't we all strive to be welcomed and accepted? Even if we are doing so unconventionally, as even when we are choosing to not conform, there is a sense that we would like to be respected or at least accepted for our choices. Yet, are we modelling a life of acceptance? Are we accept*ing*? This is the first port of call to accepting others, situations and events. However, firstly we must accept ourselves and in this way, we are 'setting the scene' for acceptance in our life.

By offering a framework and not a prescription, I congruently express that the best artwork is the one where you place yourSELF at the centre – not the version of you that is governed by the 'shoulds' imposed by society but the one that is deep inside. I know from experience that when we allow the voice of that inner self to lead the way, we paint the most beautiful art, as we create the most beautiful life, both personally and professionally.

Step into your Magnificence

I have a wealth of self-development exposure, yet it took me years for me to follow through with what I knew to be true for my growth. This life is a revolving cycle. One would assume that most of us know that to know and not do, is a painful reality, like the 'hound dog laying on the nail', as told by Les Brown, Iyanla Vansant and Lisa Nichols. Acting on what we know takes an investment in consistent action, a determination to be our genuine self and show kindness, yet in reality we will not always do right by ourSELVES. Once I started acting on my inner voice, it started to take over; it rarely lets me get away with ignoring it nowadays and most times I listen because I know my innerSELF knows me best. That is not to say that I live as though I am an island; far from it. Remember connecting with kindred souls is our fuel to increased growth and capacity. What it means though, is that my innerSELF is much more discerning than the self that allowed me to be governed by the 'shoulds' and expectations of others; the one that was driven by a strong, 'People pleasing' driver.

The last few years, in the process of cultivating my own colours, I have let my inner self guide me away from relationships, job roles and contracts that my bank balance needed; however, my heart and soul did not resonate with. I have learned to let my heart lead, as this is where the best version of self is painted. I do not claim that this is easy and I certainly do not subscribe to the, "if I can, you can" mantra as I find that to be too dismissive. Everything is relative and we are all walking our own unique paths, so my baseline advice is to start from where you are and try not to engage in too much comparison with what others are doing.

With that in mind, my framework for growing your colours and stepping into your magnificence, is a guide, a map, or in non-metaphoric terms, simply some ideas to help you along the way. This is not one-size-fits-all and requires patience and tenacity, ideally accompanied with some mentoring too, depending upon how invested you are in growing your colours. I am of the mind that if it takes ten days, ten weeks, ten months or ten years, the learning along the way is priceless, which is why I champion the scenic route. This is especially so, if your journey is fuelled by that essential ingredient, 'reflection' – the first port of call in my framework, which I have summarised here by highlighting my top ten action points to get you started.

A Framework for Growing Your Colours

1. **Reflection** – Journaling is a great way to reflect and muse over one's life. If writing a journal is not for you, use the audio record function on your phone, to record your reflections and identify patterns and cycles. Do not be afraid to look *in on* yourself, to look *at* yourself and remember to take an, "I am okay" perspective, even when seeing things that you would like to change.

2. **Find your friends** – whether in books, audiobooks, via YouTube video learning or online forums, find out who your *she*roes and

*he*roes are and rather than worship them, sit alongside them and engage in meaningful 'making' of your own life.

3. **Prayer changes everything** – It took many years for me to give myself over to God. My ego would not let go, even though I considered myself a spiritual being. My assumption had always been that prayer and worship would restrict my life. In fact, the opposite has happened and my experience has been one of liberation. Even for those who do not believe in God, having a sense of a greater, vaster universal influence, enables us to put our own existence into perspective.

4. **Meditation is a must** – It can take time to carve out the quiet space, however it is worth it. There are many types of meditation, so if the notion of sitting in silence fills you with dread, or feels like an unrealistic endeavour, there are alternatives to explore if you choose to.

5. **Seek guidance** – Whether from trusted colleagues, friends, mentors, from God or the source, seek guidance. Actively ask the questions that need answering in your life. Seeking guidance, whether through prayer, meditation or introspection, or whatever it is that reveals to you a sense of purpose, a sense of validation and direction. This activates

senses that offer a 'red or green-light system' and right action becomes clear.

6. **Visualise** – The bridge between vision and reality. You need to attach feelings and emotion to whatever you seek, so that what you visualise starts to take on three-dimensional features and starts to *feel real within the physical plane,* starts to feel *your vibration now*. Quiet time and meditation can help you to focus in on your vision and visua*lise* it as a reality.

7. **Vision board** – Seeing what you want to attract into your life, in all its technicolour, is extremely powerful. I have come across some great approaches to vision boards, using the concept of Feng-Shui and a grid called the 'Ba Gua Grid', which conveys a clear way to organise your vision board. It is amazing how three-dimensional your goals become, once you prioritise them on your vision board. There is nothing to lose, so give it a go and enjoy the process. Create your vision board, place it by your bedside and meditate on it day and night. You would be surprised what can materialise in your life.

8. **Move with Purpose** - Gaining a sense of the bigger picture can sometimes confuse, deceive and can even convince us that what we are

doing is somehow incorrect. At some point, the purposeful professional will make bold moves that may attract the doubters and critics. It is crucial to remain steadfast and focussed on the bigger picture. My advice is to play it forward to the life you want to achieve and know you deserve.

9. **Taking right action, listening and responding** - Right action may not be a grand gesture, such as immediately handing in your notice and booking the next ticket to a remote geographical area! Right action for a purposeful professional may mean starting a course of research to understand how to deepen knowledge of the next necessary step. It could mean putting it 'out there' by sharing your vision.

10. **Mind Map** – ConsultaChameleon as a career path, began as a mind map, I created on my iPad, as I sat by the river Thames one day, although it is rooted in my childhood, which is another story! I emptied my mind and began the process of bringing all my skills to the table. Being focused in one place has shown me how I can spread my skills far and wide.

That was in 2013 and I have not looked back since, unless of course to acknowledge how far I have come!

Reflection Zone:

1. What five things do you need to ditch, in order to step out of the monochrome life?

2. What three actions could you take right now, to grow your colours?

3. What three things did you enjoy as a child?

4. What are the three ways that you could tune into your right brain?

5. What are three things you have 'in your hands' right now, that you could build on?

6. What does freedom look like to you?

7. What are five ways, or areas of your life, where you are living out of alignment?

8. What are five ways that you could improve your alignment?

9. What would your life look like, if you threw all the 'shoulds' in the rubbish bin?

10. What does a magnificent life look like for you?

Ruth Pearson

Leadership and Wellbeing Coach and Trainer

www.listeningtoyourvoice.co.uk

"Listen to your inner voice, and do not let anyone stop you from being the person you know, within, you need to be."

Ruth Pearson

Step Out of Your Comfort Zone

Filling Up Your Cup

How would you describe your perspective on life? Is your glass of life, half full or half empty? Are you an optimist, or a pessimist? I believe the way you view yourself goes a long way in how you treat yourself and allow others to treat you. For many, these decisions are subconscious, as affirming and thinking positively about ourselves, are not strategies and skills we normally engage in. In fact, people who promote themselves in a positive way, are often described as being vain or very egotistical.

I have worked in education for more than 30 years and fully realise that although the system prepares learners for passing examinations, little time is given to teaching life-coping strategies. These build resilience to handle setbacks, with a positive outlook for the challenges learners will face in their lives, such as sickness, unemployment, long-term illnesses of family members and death of a loved one.

In the United Kingdom, individuals are taught to keep emotions buried and therefore this attitude has been found to impact mental health and wellbeing. For some medical conditions, the root cause of illness is due to unresolved challenges, that seem surmountable. We learn that it is fine to talk about physical challenges, however, when they are emotional or due to our mental health and wellbeing, there is still a stigma. Although things have improved over the last few years, as many famous people have now come out and shared about how they have battled with depression, anxiety, eating disorders or self-harming, there is still not enough help available. You can have all the money in the world, yet still feel worthless and desperately unhappy.

In July 2013, my life headed down a road I never would have anticipated. I was made redundant from the school I was working in and I felt as if the five years of hard work and sacrifices, had gone straight down the drain. I felt devastated and wondered what my future would hold. I was the sole Deputy Head Teacher in a secondary school and therefore had to carry out many leadership roles, at the same time as teaching science and maths. I was also completing my Master's degree in Education, researching how coaching could be used as a tool for school improvement, so I did not anticipate it would have been so difficult to gain another leadership role.

Several applications were made, including telephone interviews, however no interviews in schools were forthcoming. I decided to find myself a leadership coach and a current Head Teacher, to work with me to complete the application forms, yet every time they would ask when the interviews was, I would reply, "*I have not been shortlisted.*" For someone who was optimistic in life, I became very pessimistic and my self-confidence hit an all-time low.

Eventually, I was offered a role to be a potential middle leader in a school. It was difficult working in this school, as I did not really feel accepted, valued, or part of the team. I had a few members of staff who were supportive, however life was lonely there and I often wondered if this was the purpose God had for my life. I was given another opportunity to take up a leadership role in Deal, in the Kent area. This was the first time for me, to work away from home during the week and come home at weekends. This role had many challenges, which sadly took a toll on my health. One day I was at work teaching, the next day I was being admitted into a local hospital, having a lupus flare up. I spent three weeks in hospital, my longest time, followed by several months recuperating. If I am being really honest with myself, it was a very difficult time in my life because I felt isolated and alone.

As I look around today and see all the challenges many are facing, due to the pandemic, it brings back many memories of this time in my life. One day you are at work being a successful decision-maker and the next, you are having to face the bias and prejudice of others, including a loss of identity and self-worth. If you can relate to this story, then you too will understand the difficulties faced when adapting to new circumstances.

I eventually went back to work in another school and was looking forward to things being different. I was not prepared for the challenges I would face, which resulted in me having an emotional meltdown one day at work. I truly now felt my world had completely fallen apart. One day, I was in the classroom teaching and the next day I was in my doctor's surgery, wondering how I had gotten there, as I sat on a chair, uncontrollably crying my eyes out and feeling completely distraught. My doctor was concerned about my wellbeing, as he had never seen me like this in the ten plus years I had been his patient. He referred me to what I now know was the emergency mental health services. I realise this was the best decision he could have made because it opened unexpected doors for me. I would never have imagined coming home and picking up a journal, let alone to write how I was feeling on a regular basis. Getting my feelings out on to paper became my saviour. I asked myself the question, *"Why can people have the same opportunities, however their outcomes in life be so different?"* It was not fair.

I remember my first therapy session. I was informed I could talk for as long I needed, to start to gain some clarity. I had their undivided attention, for over an hour and this was not something I was used to. As we spoke, I was now able to understand myself in a new way. I did not need to be strong all the time and it was important I allowed others into my life who would support me. For the next eighteen months, I had a variety of therapies, including group sessions, mindfulness classes and individual therapy sessions. The more I attended the sessions, the more I realised there was a gap in the education system, in the way we are taught to look after our own mental health and wellbeing. This gap, I started to address with the development of my own coaching and training programme, which I now call 'Empowering Transformations: *To Bring Out Your Greatness Within'*. I learned several valuable lessons, including, *"You cannot fill up the cups of others, before filling up your own cup"*. Otherwise, you will end up thirsty, in the quest for knowledge.

Facing Your Fears
Since I was a child, I have always been very independent. When knocked down, I would pick myself up and continue through life. This current chapter in my life was very new because I would have to allow others into my personal space, in order to achieve the inner healing I needed. I remember being in one of the group sessions, where the women were sharing why they were in therapy. One by one, they were breaking down crying. Crying in public was not something I did. When it came to my turn, I felt myself picking up the clipboard, we had to make notes on and placing it in front of my face and refusing to continue with the session. After the session, I called my therapist and as we spoke, I realised for the first time, I needed help if I was going to heal from all the pain I had been carrying, including from my childhood scars. I had to be bold and make the decision to step outside of my comfort zone.

At this time, I had another fear to overcome; was I going to return to teaching, or look for a new occupation? Whilst I was home still recuperating, following my meltdown, I carried out a career skills audit, which resulted in the suggestion that I would make a good Coach and Trainer, with the skills I had acquired from the education sector. I bravely took the plunge and left teaching to start up my own business, 'Listening To Your Voice Ltd.' I went on a journey to find out from those in the business sector, what was missing from the education system.

I attended several networking events and learnt new skills. I learnt how to pitch why I thought it was important for employers to look after the wellbeing of their staff. It was really difficult at first because I was not used to having to talk about myself and my skillset in this way, to people who were not from an educational background; I was required to deliver my message in a different way. Remember, I had spent my whole life within an education setting and now I was completely out of my depth. There were many occasions when I just wanted to close my business; however, in those times, I would meet somebody who would give me the word of encouragement I needed, to keep pursuing my goals. I eventually joined a Female Founder's group and received the business support I really needed.

I was fortunate to get a mentor from JP Morgan, as part of this programme hosted by Enterprise Enfield, and become one of their programme Ambassadors. My mentor helped me to understand I had a warm depth inside of me and a variety of skills I could share with others, as a business owner. This was a turning point in my life, as it allowed me the opportunity to overcome the fears I was facing on a daily basis. I was able to develop my coaching and training model, to the extent that I started to get coaching clients and more speaking opportunities.

Following the attendance at the business show and taking part in a speed-networking event, I was referred to a businessman, Ian, who would open the doors for me to be part of the new project, 'Good News Britain'. I became a television presenter for a community project and I came out of my comfort zone once more. I was given the opportunity to speak about things that really mattered to my core values, as well as serving my local community. This was the launch of my media skills and becoming a professional public speaker.

Why am I sharing these personal experiences with you? I want you to know that even though in life you may have setbacks and challenging times may come your way, always be aware that you can use these setbacks as stepping-stones to a new destiny.
My wilderness time, as I call these years of planting my roots in a new business, taught me so many skills. I networked with people from a variety of business

backgrounds. I learnt a whole load of information from people, as they shared their pitches at networking events I attended. I soon realised I had a talent of being able to share my coaching and training programme in a variety of niches because of the skills I had learned as a teacher, on how to differentiate or adapt my teaching, to suit the needs of the learners. The way I explained this to others was using the example of teaching the subject of 'plants' to a five-year-old and then extending this same knowledge to meet the needs of an 18-year-old biology student, having to complete an essay on how the plant functions, using the process of photosynthesis as part of their A-level examinations.

I met the Publisher, Winsome Duncan, in February of 2017, at a business event at the Millennium Gloucester Hotel in Chelsea. At this time, I was finishing the manuscript for my second book, *'Say Yes to New Opportunities: Be Motivated to L.E.A.R.N'*. This self-help book links together motivation, holistic wellbeing and leadership skills, with activities for the reader to put their learning into practice. From this book, I realised I had a new calling over my life. I was no longer just a Teacher. Now, I was becoming an expert in the fields of personal and leadership development, all because I had become an author. This was an exciting time for me because I was becoming more confident in approaching and delivering to audiences across London. I felt like I was living on my purpose.

Embracing the Calling on your Life

I was at a new junction in my life and had some difficult decisions to make. How could I combine my experiences as a teacher, with the new roles of being a Coach and Trainer? I also had another decision to make, due to events which had taken place in 2014 after having to spend several months recuperating after the worst flare up of my lupus. During this time, I had started writing my first book, a devotional works, *'Listening for God's Voice'*. I had the opportunity to attend a women's retreat called Overcoming Emotional Baggage and to share some of my writing with the women who were attending. Two weeks before this event, I took sick again and ended up back in the hospital, in a lot of pain, wondering if I would survive this flare up. I felt afraid, as my future looked bleak. I was discharged on the Thursday night, and made the decision to attend the retreat, on the Friday. I shared three devotional writings that weekend:

- Listening to your voice
- Be a good witness
- Refreshed and restored

These three devotionals outlined what happened to all who attended that weekend and another seed was planted, with another step taken outside of my comfort zone. I had left home on the Friday, unable to walk, being fully supported by others and I came back home walking independently on Sunday. The miracle which took place that weekend transformed my life in ways I never fully understood, until 2020. It showed me that with the right atmosphere and people around me, I was able to be fully healed.

Like many have experienced, 2020 took its toll on my life. I sadly lost several family members, not due to Covid-19 and had to spend the majority of the year at home shielding, due to being on the clinically extremely vulnerable government list.

How was I going to use this time in a productive way? First, I became a Corporate Mental Health Facilitator, to integrate their training with my Empowering Transformations course. I then adapted a faith-based book I had written the previous year. Once completed and edited, my Editor, Linda, advised me to find a publisher for the book. I contacted Winsome straight away and shared with her the journey I had been on for the last few months. She offered me an opportunity I never would have dreamed of; she showed me what was possible. Instead of just publishing my book, *'Home at Last: Your Journey of Faith in Challenging Times'*, Winsome reflected on the conversation we had had in 2017 and she advised me on becoming a publishing company. Following further conversations, I took up this challenge to move completely out of my comfort zone and Listening to Your Voice Publishing, was birthed. Winsome saw the passion I had for literature all those years ago and she saw something in me that I did not see in myself at the time. What made this opportunity even more remarkable, was the logo I had from my parent business, 'Listening To Your Voice' was suitable for the publishing company, as it is a book with three butterflies coming out of the pages. How fitting and on point this was.

As more and more people shared their personal experiences of what they were going through, due to the pandemic and the changes in their identity, I realised all of the experiences and the journey I had been through for the last five years was preparing me for this calling on my life. I was now able to combine all of my experiences, within my programme, Empowering Transformations.

All of these experiences aligned with the butterflies' life cycle. At first, they are just like an egg, insignificant in the world. The egg becomes a caterpillar, eating away in their small known area. They then go into a dark place, into a cocoon (similar to the womb). It is in here that metamorphosis takes place and transformation unclips its wings. I have learned that it is here that the past has to be left behind, to make room for the future. The day arrives when they emerge as the adult butterfly. It is a difficult journey for them to break through and if they get help, they become weak and eventually die because their wings are not fully formed. This final struggle is essential for them to fully step outside of their comfort zone, to become the beautiful butterfly which they always were.

Inside of each one of us, is a beautiful butterfly which needs to emerge. The question is, are we prepared to go on the journey to allow the inner butterfly to emerge? I help my clients take this journey. I share with them strategies as to how they can improve a variety of areas of their life, using the mnemonic S.T.E.P.S.

What does S.T.E.P.S. stand for?
- **S** = Start – You need to have a starting point in your journey.
- **T** = Team - Who do you have to support you? What personal and professional roles do you have?
- **E** = Empowerment – How do you take back control of your life?
- **P** = Positive Mindset - Why is it important to have a growth mindset, instead of a fixed one?
- **S** = Success - Why should we celebrate the big and small achievements in our lives?

Where am I now in my journey? I have been on a journey where my new approach to life takes up the place of my stretch and panic zones, as conceptualised in 1908, via what is known as Yerkes–Dodson law. I realise, if I had not been on such a difficult emotional journey the last seven years, I would not be the individual I am today. I have a Divine inner peace because I realise I am pursuing God's calling on all areas of my life. I am able to impact the lives of others in a positive way because I am able to empathise with the journey they are currently travelling on. I know

now, the importance of managing my stress levels effectively.

I have learned it is imperative to step out of our comfort zones, even if we are feeling fearful. As we move on up, we meet individuals, who may come back into our lives years later and be key influences in helping us to reach the calling that God has in our lives. Let me end with the quote from one of my books. *"Listen to your inner voice, and do not let anyone stop you from being the person you know within, you need to be."*

At first, I thought it was others who were stopping me from achieving my success, however now I realise that the greatest barrier was myself. Do not let yourself be your greatest hindrance from being the person you know within you need to be. Step out of your comfort zone today and be bold. As you go you will make a big difference in the lives of others, in more ways than you ever would have imagined. This has been my experience and I know it can be your story and your experience too. Your time is now.

Reflection Zone:

1. When you were a child, what did you want to be when you became an adult and why?

2. Go somewhere peaceful, with a blank piece of paper and some stationery and draw a beautiful picture of your ideal life. What did you draw?

3. What are three things you are proud you have achieved today? Write them down in a journal, or on your phone. Do this at least three times a week and reflect on your growth. Be gentle with yourself.

4. Carry out an audit on how well you are looking after your physical wellbeing, on a scale of 1-10, with 1 being low and 10 high. Consider, are you getting enough rest, exercise, sunshine, fresh air and water?

5. For each of the areas highlighted in question four, what is one small action you can start to do, to improve your score to the next level?

6. What does the word 'empowerment' mean to you? Produce a word art poster, with the phrases and words you have selected.

7. When you are facing challenges, do you use the phrase, "I can" or "Can I"? Give an example of the impact of using each phrase.

8. What are some activities which you carry out now, that are in your comfort zone?

9. What are some activities which you could achieve, if you just stepped outside of your comfort zone into your stretch zone?

10. What are some activities that you would love to do, if you could handle your inner fears and doubt, which are now in your panic zone?

Anna B. Sexton

Artist, Social Entrepreneur and Enterprise Facilitator

www.opentocreate.com

"Never doubt that a small group of thoughtful, committed, citizens can change the world. Indeed, it is the only thing that ever has."

Margaret Mead

Be Open To Create...

Now is the time to read, digest and play with your own self-concept around your inner creative self. Over the years of playing with, working on and developing myself as an artistic and creative human-being, it has become apparent to me that, "You do not have to be an artist to be creative".

This is the motto that now underpins my own development of my creative muscles and the work I do alongside a range of people from all walks of life. The archetype of the artist is just one of many manifestations of creativity.

I am the Founder of an innovative social enterprise called, 'Open To Create...'. We work with individuals on a quest to find out how to maximise their creative potential and organisations who want their staff and teams to become more creative in their daily outputs, have more fun and play in the roles they do each day. My role is to act as a signpost, to hold the door open and invite you to connect more deeply to what is truly creative about you, your outlook on life and how you want to share your creative gifts and talents in the world.

You may not have picked up a future paintbrush and that is okay. Picking up a brush, pen or an instrument may be your thing; equally it might be a spatula, a chisel or ball.

Below I have crafted out a manifesto to inspire you to nurture your own unique creative talent and grow yourself into a more robust and sustainable, artistic human.

My hope is that these prompts and accompanying questions, will guide you to become more at ease and make peace with the awe of your creativity...
Let us begin...

1. Believe you are creative – this really is one of the biggest barriers to exploring, experimenting and letting your creative self blossom.

2. Everyday creativity is found in seeing what you do and how you do it on a day-to-day basis. You may already notice that there are times in your life already, that you find you have imaginative ideas and thoughts – is there a pattern of when those times are? Or have you noticed particular moments? For example, many people get their best inspiration in the bathroom during a shower, a run, driving or washing up. These periods of time are when we are tapping into ways of being and doing familiar sets of steps, that have almost become second nature to us. Start to notice when and what gets you most in flow and then listen in, to hear what creative things you are dreaming of making a reality.

Having a notebook and pen nearby your bed or in a bag you use most days, is a great way to capture any thoughts you have throughout the day or week. See it like being a detective looking for creative clues.

3. Open up to what is inside of you - find ways that you may be blocking your creativity through limiting beliefs, for example:
"I am not creative."
"I am too old to be playful and have fun."
"It is too silly or frivolous to begin that creative idea I have always wanted to try."

Take some quiet time to let yourself 'listen' into your thought-blockers and any visions that come to mind, as ways that you halt yourself creatively. Be honest, loving and kind with yourself, as you uncover these gems. Knowing what blocks us, is as important as what drives our creative vision forward.

Write down on a piece of paper or a note-taking app, what it is you would let yourself try out or do more of, if you had the time and could let go of the blockages that obstruct your path to creation. Even if the idea is not fully formed yet, try drawing a map on a scrap piece of paper with pens, which allow you to play more, before your ideas becoming more defined. This will act as the mind map to guide you forward; words, pictures, symbols, any way you like to get ideas out of your head works. You can even include the stumbling blocks on the map, however, create ways around them in your own way.

4. Perspective is key – now you are starting to come up with ideas for creative projects, or actions you want to take. It is vital to look at what you want to make from as many angles as you possibly can. Get thinking beyond what is initially visually in front of you and what is obvious. These new ideas are precious and tender, like a seedling when it is growing in the soil during the early stages of spring. Your ideas need tending in the same way the seedlings need soft, gentle rain, shelter and sunshine to help them grow more robust and stronger. This process can often be supported by sharing your idea or vision with a suitably supportive friend, colleague, or family member. Suitable means you know you can trust them to actively listen and they can guide you by giving you the type of perspective you are seeking.

5. Engage as fully as you can with the artistic process you are in. It will not be linear and that is okay; it will not be in any way 'perfect' and most of all, it will constantly expand. The more you broaden your perspective around your inner creativity, the more your horizons will extend. Dip in and out of this manifesto and question as it suits you or go through each step, one by one. You get to choose what works best.

6. Nuance is there in all things, specifically around knowing yourself and the ways you like to create and bring ideas to life. Maybe you are more of a 'one idea at a time person', so give yourself the time to delve into each of the ideas and look for all the subtle ways they can each be developed, grown or discounted. Editing out ideas matters as much as keeping them in. Try to remain in your free-flow without inhibitions. Maybe you are more of a, 'I have one idea and would love to work that up' type of person. This is fantastic, your role here is to also dig into that one idea from as many angles as possible and rigorously question this one idea, which will make it even stronger and robust in the long run. However you creatively think, there are always more ways to look at your process and test your assumptions.

7. Translate what you discover through your own creative language. This can seem a bit much if you are starting out on your creative path, so link how you like to experience the world to what is going to get the most out of you creatively. Do you like to *see* things, or are you a more tactile person, learning through feeling your way into something? Or do you like to listen to others and this inspires you? Maybe taste or smell is key for you? Everyone is different and unique. Your role is to act as detective to uncover what your own creative language is and be open to be surprised. The key here, is stepping beyond anything others have told you about yourself in your life. So many people had a teacher, parent or carer, who said something 'throw-away' and glib about, "not being good at drawing or singing" and this can be another form of blockage, to really knowing your artistic and creative language.

8. Organise yourself in ways that uniquely suit who you are and what you require. Some people love an ordered approach to creativity and others like a more random, 'follow their nose' approach. The great thing about creativity, is that you get to do it your way. Be self-taught or go study. Read a book or keep a sketch book near your desk or bedroom stand. Listen to podcasts and bake bread. Run and listen to children's audio books or watch cartoons. Do whatever it takes to bring out the inner child that wants to play.

9. Create as regularly as you can -make, flop, scrunch up, try again, fail fast, fail forward, take it slow, speed it up, cut and paste, be inspired and repeat. The most important thing is to seek out what inspires you daily and keep doing that and if that starts to stop inspiring you, try something else. Be like the wind, flow and ebb as you explore your artistic strengths. Creativity is very much like any muscle; once you start to flex it, the energy grows to propel you forward to do more and it can be in the most micro of step-by-step ways. The thing to watch is your head getting into telling you big is better. No creative idea, vision or project starts off big. The seed is watered and grows to the exact right size you need it to be. Over time, you start to sense when your 'creative something' is done.

10. Review with kindness, care and honesty what is working for you and delighting you. Equally be mindful of being too quick to judge a creative idea or piece as 'rubbish', 'ugly' or 'too over done'. Keep a folder or have a place to keep your creative treasures, as you can then return to them at a later date and you may very well be surprised to find your opinion radically alters. If physical space is an issue, create a digital place that suits who you are, where all your ideas, work and/or projects are stored, so you have the chance to revisit them when you need to. For example, a folder in your photo gallery, just for snaps of your works in progress. Plus, this gives your mind a noticeably clear way to track your progress and it is useful if, down the line, you need to or want to share any of your creative results.

11. Excite yourself about all the progress you are making. Eventually, other people may get involved or they may need to be, if linked to a job or course you are taking. However, it can be so easy to get all excited about your idea and before you know it, your mind has you setting up an Etsy store or enrolling in a year-long course to build up your creative skills. How you keep excited, inspired and driven, is to keep going whatever the outcomes are. Taking your creative self by the hand and making gentle steady progress, is way more manageable than taking giant leaps that your creative self will not thank you for.

12. Acknowledge yourself in all progress you are making and be of good cheer. You are invited from the get-go to build in time to uplift, care, champion and celebrate the progress you are making; end of, no exceptions. This needs to underpin the creative journey you are on, doubly reinforced as a strong foundation of self-esteem and the resilience to keep going. It may be that you share your creative outputs with others and their feedback will be important. However, from now on, if you steady yourself with your truthful, kind and caring inner guiding voice, those times when feedback is critical and harsh, you will be more flexible, like a young tree blowing in the wind.

13. Take time out to go beyond where you are in the moment. Creativity ebbs and flows, like all forms of energy and time away from a creative idea or project allows for perspective to be gained. Resting allows for recharging your inner batteries, restoring balance and filling up your cup, once you have made huge outputs. It is ok to take a step back, see the project afresh or a look at the piece from all angles to see what way feels the right way up, or even to decide to shelve it for a longer period, before returning to it. I often have two or three projects going on at the same time, as this gives me the choice to move back and forth between the ones I am most drawn to in the moment. Variety is the spice of life.

14. Examine what is next. All creative processes, approaches and projects have cycles. By building in key points to evaluate and make decisions about what is next, you can keep a clear steer of your own creative ship regardless of whether the work is purely for your fun and delight or for a client. This can sometimes be easier when an idea or project is for someone else, via work or a client. Be honest with yourself, as many of us abandon our creative dreams and goals for the multitude of distractions available to us via family, friends, work or study or volunteering commitments. Have boundaries and schedule in time with yourself, to keep your creative journey core to all your other commitments and over time, you will really feel and see the incremental or larger changes you are making.

Reflection Zone:

1. What can you see, hear, or feel around you, that reflects back your creativity?

2. What are the creative choices you are already making in your life? Make a record of your findings in a way, or ways that best suit who you are as a person.

3. What blockages did you discover that are literally or metaphorically preventing your own creative path to becoming more open to create?

4. How could you reframe the blockages into building blocks, or 'leaping off' points?

5. In building a timeline of actions and ideas that are ready to begin and prioritise, what five things would you list?

6. Where can you build a 'space' for yourself to honour your new-found creativity?

7. Who do you know that inspires you to be more creative? Write a list of 15 people (alive, dead or fictional). Once you have your list, write next to each name what it is about them that inspires you.

8. Start an acknowledgement jar or box, to keep mementos that inspire your creativity.

9. How could you carve out up to one hour of your time each week, to be more creative?

10. Who do you know, who could support and guide you to the next level?

Patricia Bidi

Printmaking Linocut Art

www.patriciabidi.com

"I travel through the things I research and create. It's an adventure."

Patricia Bidi

The Art of Transforming Your Life

The moment I realised something had to change, it was at the hospital A&E department. When the doctor told me that he could not find anything abnormal in my tests, I felt unsettled. An ambulance had brought me there because I had unbearable pain in my legs, I felt dizzy and I was unable to walk. This happened after many months of going to the doctor for various ailments and problems. He gave me strong painkillers to ease my pain. I was totally confused, until I finally realised that I was in so much pain because I was in an unhappy situation and my life was not going in the direction I wanted. I felt suffocated and I was not being real, authentic and honest with myself.

It was at that moment in the waiting room, that I began to get clear about what I did not want for the rest of my life. I decided to open my eyes to the harsh reality that was my life. I asked for guidance, clues and signs and I started to reflect on my life, up until that moment. The following week I was in pain again and I went to the GP, however this time I was ready to pay attention to everything that would help me towards my healing process. I felt that I had to take responsibility for my experience and my own healing and not wait on a doctor's magic pill to make everything better. I felt that I had to have the courage to learn more about myself.

As soon as Dr Fox opened the door, I paid attention to him immediately and to what was surrounding him in his office. He greeted me warmly, with a smile. Out of the corner of my eye, I saw something that caught my attention. It was a beautiful painting on the wall that I had never seen before. I forgot what I had come for this time and I asked him about the painting, who painted it and so many more inquisitive questions. He said that it was a painting by Wassily Kandinsky, that he had seen in the Museum of Modern Art in New York. This was an animated moment that reawakened something in me, it fed my curiosity, my love for exploration and learning; something that had been left on the back burner for a long time.

After that, I went straight to my local library located in front of my GP practice and started to explore all these painters, starting with Kandinsky. After many weeks of research, I had this intuitive instinct to start drawing again. I also began making tiny changes in my life. At the beginning, they were all temporal. As I enjoyed my new moments more, I kept making more changes, until they became permanent. This made a dramatic change to my health and wellbeing. I found the courage to change my perspective and take responsibility for the pain and healing process. Soon after, I stopped visiting my GP because I didn't have any more complaints.

I started permitting myself to do the things I loved, at first taking small steps, one at a time. Starting to make art and play with my imagination, not only gave me a break from my everyday life but I became lighter, happier and healthier. I started noticing beauty in unexpected places, creating, experimenting with colours and I started to have more playtime fun with my children too. Being creative helped me to become more intuitive; I often felt led and started to encounter meaningful coincidences daily. To change my life, I had to take responsibility for my healing and take small steps. This is what empowered and fuelled my personal growth.

As I started being more authentic, I started doing the things I loved, despite all kinds of obstacles. That gave me the courage to regain my freedom, believe in myself and understand my nature as a spiritual being. Being 'present', helped me to realise the changes that I needed to make. The passion to create and the constant process of self-discovery, gives me freedom and inspiration to transmute, knowing that personal transformation is needed, to make this world a better place.

Persistence in creativity

Reflecting to a time painting in my first studio in Sydenham, I recall that the colours of the painting were clashing in this particular piece. I was getting tired of the painting and I wanted to move on and start a new one; however, I had to finish it for an exhibition and I had a deadline, so I persevered. In the end, after making numerous changes over many weeks, it became clear that it was the best piece of work that I had ever done. It inspired me so much I wanted it to be with me after the exhibition; however, it sold on the day of the private view. The same happened with my first oil painting entitled, 'Red World'. I started painting with layers of egg tempera and it shifted into oil painting at the end.

There were many times when I was resistant to finishing a piece of art or project I had been working on, where I was thinking it was not coming together. I could see it was not the colour, texture and unity that I wanted. I could see many things were not working with it and I wanted to abandon the piece and start a new one because I could not see where the direction was going. That is what we do sometimes in life, we want to jump ship when the waters get rough. However, if we persevere and we do not give up, we could overcome the obstacles and grow.

In my studio many times before, I was thinking, "what I am doing here? Why do I have to put myself through this?" Something inside kept telling me to persevere and to not give up. A small, quiet voice of intuition knocked on the doors of my heart and said for me to continue. My curiosity and love for exploration and originality, would always help me to transform the painting and trust in my creative power.

When I express my creativity, follow my curiosity, my love for learning and trust my intuition, beautiful things happen. When I add life to my imagination, I can be playful and see things from a new perspective and that gives me the strength to continue. Persistence is like a vehicle that helps me to reach my destination and makes it easier to enjoy the creative process, despite the obstacles that are on the journey.

Some days I had to believe in myself, when even I doubted and questioned everything I was doing; even when nobody believed in me and people advised that I was wasting my time. Patience and persistence have been essential for my artistic work and the adversity that I have encountered, has allowed me to bring into play all the resilience from within.

Persistence has been a process of putting one of my feet in front of the other, one step at a time. First of all, I had to have the courage to start and then continue with energy and enthusiasm. I realised that transformation is easier when I have done it in small steps, when I have been flexible and detached from the outcome. When I do not have projected expectations, I can relax and let go.

When I let go of my expectations and I have patience, it means that I trust the process; I know the inspiration will come and naturally happen. When I wait for the inspiration without any anxiety, the inspiration comes to me because it finds me relaxed and it can flow through me.

Letting go helps me to be productive and explore new possibilities. It also gives me a sense of wellbeing and fulfilment, while creativity flows effortlessly. I know that if I persevere and I let go of expectations, I can allow things to happen.

The magic is in the details

Observation helps me to make unexpected connections when I am doing my work. When I pay attention to small things and details, my work is enjoyable because I am engaged with the present moment. Remembering that the present is a gift helps me to magnify the joy and magic of the present. Creation is possible when I am in the now and when feeling grateful, small things matter.

Paying attention to details does not mean aiming for perfection. As an artist, observing is important to make art. It helps me to care deeply and appreciate life. Curiosity enhances my love for learning, it helps me to see different and to find more details and ideas. When I focus my attention on a creative project, I reflect and my experience of the world is more enjoyable, enriched by its active and imaginative interpretations.

When I pay attention to details, I am in the creative zone and energy flows through me and confidence and courage improves my productivity. When I clear my mind, it is easy to focus on paying attention to the details; it is like a meditation, I can slow down and breathe. As Walt Disney said, "There is no magic in magic. It is all in the details". I can be playful and add fun and joy in my life and the life of others. It helps me to see what is important in the present moment, where everything has clarity and guides me to grow in authenticity and integrity.

Reflection Zone:

1. What are the areas you want to improve in your life?

2. What have you learned from your past mistakes?

3. How can you let go of your expectations, to enjoy the present moment?

4. Where and how can you be more creative?

5. What area of your life can you let go of; what no longer serves you?

6. In which ways can you add more value and enrich the lives of others?

7.

8. What did you enjoy as a child, that you are not enjoying now?

9. How can you accept yourself for who you are, despite your flaws?

10. What action can you take every day, towards the life of your dreams?

11. How can you look after and improve your health and wellbeing daily?

Linnette James

Author, Poet, Nurse and Motivational Speaker

LinkedIn ID: Linnette James

"My purpose is greater than my fears."

Linnette James

Racism Within the Workforce

Racism, when delivered, is a form of abuse. It is an abuse that can evoke both emotional and psychological trauma. It can be frightening, stressful and can limit, if not destroy, the self-esteem or belief of an individual.

Racism, when experienced, does not just touch the surface of an individual's emotions. Rather, it pierces the soul of the person on the receiving end and can be destructive, causing the stain to stay with the recipient for a lifetime.

If you are in doubt, look at the aftermath of George Floyd's death, Rest in Peace. For months, people of minoritized ethnic origin, protested. They protested because they could identify with his experience. So many untold stories were narrated, by famous names and faces. The pain of the experiences that were told, were apparent on the faces of these individuals, even though some of the traumas occurred years ago. The bottom line is that pain is colourless, however it still travels globally.

We look at the pandemic and the reports of key workers, particularly those working within the field of nursing. For the first time in It is history, the NHS was so openly and heavily criticised for its racial discrimination of its employees, during a pandemic.

As an immigrant who has lived in Britain for the past 27 years, worked in the NHS for 16 years, across different services and as a published author for the past 16 years, I have a wealth of experience and exposure with different age groups, races, gender and individuals from a variety of backgrounds and status in life. Some of these exposures have come with challenges, in the form of institutionalised racism and discrimination within the work environment. Some of the approaches can be easily identified and given the scope to challenge, as they are so brutal and open in their approaches. However, others are so shrouded, you would need the defence of a consultant psychiatrist, to declare that you are mentally stable, should you dare to challenge the behaviour of the perpetrators.

The profession is meant to be caring, ultimately saving many lives, designed to help to heal the sick and restore individuals, who through developing an illness or disease, have experienced a change in character, or lost their optimum level of functioning; therefore, one would make certain assumptions. Yes, one would assume that such an establishment would extend a duty of care to all mankind, regardless and irrespective of their differences. One could also assume that such a culturally-rich institution would promote equality and celebrate diversity throughout all its ranks. After all, to be a carer or giver, this must be embedded in one from birth, nurtured through their environment and enhanced with three years of Nurse training.

To witness someone with far less skills and experience than you be promoted and to then be asked to train this person, who has been given a role that you could do with your eyes closed, is quite frankly debilitating.

To be given tasks and roles that are deemed of higher risk, more challenging and less appealing to that of your Caucasian colleagues, is outrageous.

To be given a lesser time scale to complete the same task that has been given to your Caucasian colleagues, is unjust.

To have less of an opportunity to access training that your Caucasian colleagues can so easily access, is unfair.

To witness the dismissal or ridicule of your colleague who tries in vain to get her point across, every time she attempts to speak in a meeting that is designed for staff to be heard' is diabolical.

To see management, alongside your fellow Caucasian colleagues, successfully orchestrate a witch hunt against you or your fellow colleague of colour, should be unheard of.

To be treated as if you simply do not belong, as if you are invisible, is unacceptable.

Yet, it would appear that no one wants to talk about it and they remain hidden by the traditional 'stiff upper lips' and stuffy walls.

When you have witnessed your fellow black colleague being told to get up from a laptop in the most disrespectful manner by a Caucasian, so she could use it instead because she thinks she has more of a right to have access to NHS property, is just cruel.

When you have heard that your black colleague was dismissed with the wave of a hand, by a fellow colleague, who is Caucasian and demanded to, "get out of my presence!" is reminiscent of still being on the master's plantation fields, picking cotton in Mississippi.

All these are done without the use of the "N" word, which was so frequently used in making reference to our forefathers. They were done without you being on a plantation owned by slave masters. They were done without the breath physically leaving your body. However, they carry the same effect as a foot on your neck in 2021.

One might ask, "how and why do you call this racial discrimination?"

Well, if it is not racial discrimination, what is it? Racism can be direct and indirect, hidden and in plain sight.

Some might even use the term, "unconscious bias", to describe the heinous act.

If my skin and the skin tone of my fellow black colleagues were not so mocha in its hue, then maybe we could get by on light-skinned lineage. If our features were less of our African ancestors and more like the Caucasian masters who forced themselves on our fore parents, who bore their children, then maybe we would be acceptable and meet the media's standards.

Would those within the system that choose to hand us inhumane treatment, do so if we looked like them? I used the word "choose", as every racist act is done out of choice, especially when it is overtly insensitive.

The callous acts outlined above are not a representation of my vivid imagination. They are experiences lived and witnessed, in an institution that we have seen worked tirelessly and selflessly within to save. treat and console patients and their loved ones, during an era that is unprecedented. We are still getting cracks on backs; it is just disguised better.

How can such a beautiful institution harbour such hatred? It continues to do so because sometimes those on the receiving end, are too frightened to speak out. Those on the receiving end are sometimes so buried in self-loathing, low self-esteem and lack of self-belief, that they accept their ill-treatment as the norm. They continue on without defending themselves.

These attacks on our liberty, our integrity, our right to feel and be proud of who we are, are designed to break us, are designed to make us feel 'lesser than'.

The Value of Self Belief is a Gift

From an early age, my mother taught me to know and believe in who I am. I spent my first 16 years in Jamaica, knowing and owning who I am and not who others wanted or thought I should be. So, when I stepped off the plane at Gatwick airport in 1994, I already knew with conviction, who I was and what I was capable of achieving.

Derogatory comments and wicked attacks would not rob me of this belief, pride and self-worth my mother has instilled in me. The attacks did have an effect; it was painful, humiliating and even more so when I saw the foot of hatred and racism on the neck of George Floyd. However, I did not suffer in silence, I did not bury my experiences and the thought of running from this situation and that which I observed, never crossed my mind.

I cannot control the thought process and behaviour of others. How one conducts themselves in the privacy of their own homes, is entirely their right. However, no one has the right to impose, invade their beliefs, or what they think is their right, onto others in a public place. Especially within the work environment.

Others had gone before and did nothing. Not because they did not care but because they lacked the confidence to do so. They were frightened of the ramifications of taking on what they felt was the superior race. As they were so frightened to act, too scared to challenge the narcissists' acts, we are left to share the horrendous experiences of those before us, in sheer horror.

I had to make a change or be a part of a change. So, my fellow black colleagues and I, mobilised and fought the system! We battled because we knew we are not 'lesser than'. We overcame because we have the right to be treated with the same equality, dignity and respect that our Caucasian colleagues had bestowed on them. We stood up for ourselves because we understood that if we were being treated with such contempt and disdain, we dread the thought of what happened to our parents, our children and our sisters and brothers if they were taken ill and left at the mercy of our racist team, to provide them with care. What would happen to them?

We fought because the next generation must not tread the same path we did. We fought back because we believe in our skills, our intellectual abilities, our communication skills and the ability to make a difference. We fought and yes, we made a difference.

A small one, however one has to start somewhere, with faith as small as a mustard seed.

We were able to sit in comfort at any table with a laptop provided by the NHS and use it without any anxiety or fear. Our voices are being heard without being ridiculed or dismissed and whilst labels such as "hostile" or "angry" may be used covertly to describe our approaches, we understand that this derives from the prejudice and lack of knowledge of those who feel so threatened by our voices. So threatened are they, that they use such adjectives to describe an articulate and intelligent person, who dares to look differently.

There is a long road ahead of us. There are many more obstacles to overcome. However, we can only triumph through these barbed wires, if we have the self-belief and confidence to know how we should be treated and who we really are. We must stand firm on our truth, self-worth and values, to withstand the test of time.

No man has the right to dictate our path. The colour of our skin should not make us feel that by default, we cannot and are not a positive product of our society. If we fail to succeed, this should be by choice and not because it is expected or drilled into us that we can never make it. The colour of our skin and our beautiful features are not a curse but rather a blessing, to be rejoiced and celebrated. Our forefathers paid a price with their suffering and hard work; we must let their pain end in the past. We have read in literature of their fortitude and courage in the face of their racial struggles and the pleas of, "No Justice, No Peace". Let us celebrate our blackness, our uniqueness, our varied mocha hues and even within the institution of our recruitment, we should feel welcome and at home; for we travelled many a Windrush ship to be here!

Reflection Zone:

1. Have I remained true to myself?

2. Have I viewed the world through my own lens or that of others?

3. Have I done enough to educate others about people of my race and is it really my place to do so?

4. Did I really need to experience racism to become passionate about its plight?

5. Have I done enough to help to create a better world for our children?

6. Why is it important that I know who I am and whose I am? (God's)

7. Does my upbringing have a bearing on my view of myself?

8. Can self-belief help one to succeed against the odds?

9. Can believing in myself, cause others to feel inferior or question their worth?

10. Is my approach to empower those who are struggling with who they are and what they can achieve, the right thing to do?

Love Letters to my Younger Self

Dear little Winsome,

I wish I would have hugged you more often and told you everything will work out for your greatest good. Winnie, I have learned how to take a breath every time the wind of life left my sails. I know how to press the pause button of life, when my stress levels are raised and run free in the solitude of my serenity. My main priority is balancing my cortisol levels, which is now the order of the day, as I want to be well and live longer. Breathe deeper. Smile harder.

I wished I knew that my mantra, 'He loves me not' would become a self-fulfilling prophecy over my life. A man could never love me more until I loved myself first and that when he said goodbye, my heart would continue to beat. Embedded in me was a longing to be loved, to be held and to be validated; however, tainted love has no home here now. I hug myself at night, I love myself from the crown of my head to the soles of my feet. The scars fade, however, the overwhelming emotions stayed. I wish I knew sooner, to let go and let God and simply exhale.

What I wish I knew in my former years is, it is okay not to be okay. Rest if you must, however, do not dare quit on me now. Hold your head high and keep it moving, for a new dawn will always rise. When you close your eyes, it was biblically foretold, do not take your wrath (anger) into the next day. Pain has not come to stay; it has come but for a season and is here to teach us to be better versions of our authentic selves. Be kinder to yourself, give yourself permission to feel the entire spectrum of your emotions, sit with your tears and embrace all that ails you. I wish I knew sooner the importance of feeling your feelings, until you go through them to the other side. To learn the art of patience, by tapping into your emotional matrix. Most of all, always remember in your going out and coming in, that the present is a gift to always be mindful of.

Vibrate Higher.

Love Winsome x

Dear little Marcia,

What I wish I knew was how to deal with failure more effectively. We fail forward only to learn how not to do something. I now accept and attract the positive feedback and embrace the fact that life is a learning experience. Be kinder to yourself and have more internal and external self-awareness. I wish I understood the meaning and value of self-love and acceptance and that it is okay, not to be okay. Understanding of emotions and the importance of your feelings, means having less self-doubt and negative talk. When you know who you are, that is the foundation you must stand upon. It is okay to ask for help when required, it does not make you weak. Have more awareness of your abilities and strengths and bring it to everyday life. Learn to find your voice, let it be heard and not silenced. Rest sometimes; it is perfectly fine to break away from everything in order to concentrate on yourself as a balanced, integral individual. Get comfortable with stillness. Embrace all of you, love your imperfections without judgement and fully embrace you.

Love Marcia x

Dear little Melanie,

When I was younger, I yearned to fit in with my older step-siblings and the popular children at school, who had more freedom than I had! This led me to hide my intelligence and follow the crowd, rather than walking in my authentic truth. I was afraid to stand out and be ridiculed. I was told that I was too expressive with my hands when I spoke and that if I did not curb it, no one would focus on what I had to say. This made me feel awkward and go into my shell, sit back and wait to be asked my opinion, rather than offer it.

This meant that I excelled when someone (teacher, managers, church leaders) asked me for my opinion and input; however, if I was not pulled in, I stayed silent. It took a long time for me to find my confident self.

If I could go back in time, I would tell my younger self not to worry about what others think. That being different is a positive and that it is a great asset to be unique. I would say, "You are destined for greatness, keep your eyes on the prize and do not be distracted. The approval of others is not as important as being true to yourself. True friends will stick with you, let the fake ones go.
Just believe in you".

Love Melanie x

Dear little Shona,

What I wish I knew is that I am responsible for everything that happens in my life. When I was growing up, I never took responsibility for anything; I always blamed everyone else for the problems in my life. I never realised that the choices I was making were determining my future. In order for me to heal, find love and self-acceptance after my emotional trauma, I had to learn the art of letting go, as I held onto past hurts for so long and never forgave abusers.

I had to realise it was not about being wrong or right. Can I let you into a little secret? There is no right or wrong way, only the way you perceive life's events.
I had to start being accountable for what was in my control and face the good and bad circumstances. This in turn, freed me so I could start living, creating and most of all, walking in my God-given purpose.

I wish I knew earlier to start letting go of people, situations, places and things which tore my spirit apart. This would have given me the ability to start recreating the life I wanted sooner. I have learned not to be bound by internal pain and have now been freed. Let go of your suffering and take responsibility for every area of your life, is my greatest lesson to share. By letting go and tapping into your future, by not living in your past, you can let go and let God, move forward and own your decisions. This is when you will soar, like an eagle .Love Shona x

Dear little Joanna,

What I wish I knew was that my voice matters most, above all else. There is nothing to fear in being your authentic self and expressing who you are on this physical plane. You may die to your ego on a daily basis and you need not be held to ransom by what other people think of you. No one has to agree with you, or like what you say and you have nothing to prove to anyone else because your life is your own. You are victorious and can live in accordance with your own rules, priorities and values. At any given moment, you are free to change your mind and can become more of yourself by relinquishing the need to consider other people's views and opinions, above your own. Living this way does not make you an unkind or uncaring human being. You are only responsible for yourself and the wellbeing of your immediate family. Once you understand this principle, people-pleasing will slip away and self-care will be a guiding light.

The real love story is self-love and if you take all action in alignment with the passion and zest you have for life, you must in turn, have love for yourself. You will always make the right choices according to your life's lessons. Looking for love outside of yourself is a false economy that will bankrupt lost souls, as Lauryn Hill states, "How you gonna win, if you ain't right within?". Everything outside of you is a reflection of your inner world, so it is crucial that you prioritise taking care of yourself above all things and truly honour the temple entrusted to you. Self-love encompasses everything, including what you eat, how you live, how well you attend to your needs and then eventually, who you choose to be in relationship with. You are always having a relationship with yourself, so you must practice kindness and tolerance. These qualities must be integrated into your life authentically and not become a token of idealism.

Time is the real healer, take up the power to activate the real currency in life, as it passes quickly and there is no greater gift.

Time is a man-made illusion; we can often feel that because we have invested so much time, we have developed a stronger foundation than we actually have. This can lead us to spending yet more of our precious time on things we would be better to walk away from, sooner rather than later. Remember, time is the most precious commodity we have and cannot be refunded. Every day, you are literally spending your life. Part of our self-love anthem could be to value our cherished moments...in ALL aspects of our lives, preserving as much of this treasured exchange as we possibly can and attributing the best of it to ourselves. In being whole, the circle of life continues...

Love Joanna x

Dear little Ruth,

I am Enough!
It is only in the last few months, I have fully understood these three words, "I am enough." Everything you need to be fully happy is within you. We are made to feel we are incomplete without the latest trends, however, we soon realise these do not last for long, before the next 'good' thing arrives on the scene. Every morning when you get up, look in the mirror and say the words, "I am enough" and affirm yourself several times with conviction; let these words become you. Feel the transformation which takes place on a cellular level within.

Be Proactive
In life, opportunities are going to come your way. Some are going to be big projects; however, many will be small insignificant events, or so they may seem. As you take these small steps daily, weekly or monthly, when you look back you will see how far you have travelled from your original starting position. You will realise the 'inner you' has also changed. Things which would have previously stressed you out, no longer affect you in the same way, which can now lead you to smile, as you continue your journey to greatness.

The Practice of Patience
Have you ever looked at a house being built? First the blueprint needs to be drawn up, then a team of experts hired, before the foundations are laid. Your

body is the house of life, you need to have goals in life too; a plan which may change as the 'building' is constructed, so be sure to be flexible. The right team of construction workers must help you lay a solid foundation. Always leave it to the experts, as you cannot do everything on your own. Learn to let go and trust God. All along the process, remember you need to be patient, as no home is built in a day and the beauty comes by celebrating the small achievements along the way.

Love Ruth x

Dear little Anna,

What I wish I knew is that creativity shows up every day in many forms, from how you make choices about what outfit you wear, what music you listen to and even how you set the table.

Be willing to be pulled towards the direction of areas of interest and ways of making and creating that are new, vibrant, different or off-centre from your 'usual' activities.

Develop your 'whole' self as a person and learn what you like, what fuels your passion and observe what you do to get in your own way, that blocks your talent and leads to procrastination. Lose the distractions that inhibit you from being your most creative self.

Find your creative niche and repeatedly do what makes you happy. Mastery comes from practice.
No creative idea is perfect; what you see in your head is the guidance system, the map towards what will eventually manifest into your life.

Be okay with being flexible and fluid, with the dance of creativity. Allow for curve balls and new ideas to spring from old ideas, to build an even better version of your original idea.

Easy does it and consistency is the key to making a grand gesture investment in your innovative skillset.

Creativity compounds over time and is not easily accessible.

Be sure to use software systems, a tidy workspace, regular scheduled steps and planning really do matter, when you are a creative ball of energy. These do not thwart creativity but actually give a conduit and structure for more self-expression and for your bigger, bolder ideas to take shape.

Love Anna x

Dear little Patricia,

I wish I knew that I am responsible for everything that happens in my life and if it needs improving, I need to fix it. Attachment leads to suffering; we must strive to release what no longer serves us. No matter how bad it gets, there is always something to be grateful for; gratitude is a must. We are all united and connected on a global level, so love fearlessly. Letting go of what does not serve you works best when you understand the principle of 'surrender'. The more you give, the more you will receive. Give only to share abundance and expect nothing in return. Nothing is impossible when you focus your mind on the prize. You are powerful and resilient in good and bad times. Being in your own company allows time for reflection and allows you to grow and flourish.

Love Patricia x

Dear Little Linnette,

What I wish I knew, was the signs and when others who care about me, speak out on my behalf and express their concerns. Always think rationally, with your head and not your heart, little girl. With your intellect and never your pride or ego. They cannot all be wrong.

Please note, that not everyone forges a relationship out of love. There are people so gifted that they could win every category at the Oscars. So, be wise and if you lack the wisdom to understand the actions of others, just know that there are people that are wiser than you and one day you will become that wise sage. There are good people in the world, people who want to see you thrive, people who have sleepless nights thinking, wondering if you'll make it out alive. Always follow your inner guide.

Love Linnette x

Epilogue

In thinking about the magnificence of the process that eventually became the book, titled, *Pioneering Women Speak: Transformational Leadership on the Rise*, there is no doubt that it truly has been a transformative process. The undertone themes of our stories are rooted in accepting responsibility, whilst remaining our authentic self. It offers and promotes self-awareness, self-love and self-care, wrapped in 'feel good' proactive solutions.

As leading women, we all came together, each with our own unique insights, individual passions and aspirations, whilst embracing the creative process that grew from our organic teamwork. We were enriched through this experience and this process truly embodied the notion that the whole is greater than the sum of its parts.

As women with diverse styles, as women of colour, as women of variable spiritual persuasion, as women from a range of professional backgrounds and life situations, as female leaders, as Change Agents – we recognise the importance of what we have created in our debut anthology. Each of us have contribute our individual voice and created a symphony of voices, so that we may enthuse the reader, to recognise the leader in themselves.

The process of compiling this *Pioneering Women Speak* over a six-month period, has been creative. A well-oiled machine, carefully co-ordinated, with each author committing to a collaborative process of setting and fulfilling targets, goals and investing fully in the sisterhood that was borne from the writer's development. We had a real sense to contribute to something important and are thankful to the vision of Winsome Duncan, who is tirelessly dedicated to raising up the voices of those who are unheard and invisible.

During testing times, the process was virtual and we found ways to boost each other and maintain excitement. At the point of writing this epilogue, we are invested in sharing our knowledge and insights with our readers and the wider community, knowing that each receive messages differently and fully embracing that our diversity increases our capacity to reach significantly more people.

May this anthology transform your mindset and turbo-charge you for personal growth, that will continue to inspire and fuel your intentions, via this truly transformational experience. Keep this in mind; we know that rather than signifying the end, this epilogue is actually a symbol of new beginnings for us all.

Joanna Oliver and Winsome Duncan

About the Authors

Winsome Duncan Biography

Meet our Number One Bestselling Author and Publisher, Winsome Duncan.

Winsome Duncan is one woman, with a HUGE vision of getting her wider community writing books. She has more than 15 years' experience in the book publishing industry. As an author of 16 books, which includes her recent Amazon number one smash hit *The Popcorn House*, Winsome works tirelessly with budding Authors and Entrepreneurs, to help them realise their book-writing dreams. She is the CEO of publishing house, 'Peaches Publications' and not-for-profit social enterprise, 'the Look Like Me Book Challenge', which has a particular focus on stories and voices from the Black community, including children aged 7 – 18 years old.

Her latest project supported30 Black, Asian & Minority Ethnic (BAME) children to write one collective, community book. Since the Guardian newspaper published that a mere 5% of BAME main characters are in children's books within the UK. This is compared to 33.5% of BAME school children in education. Inanimate objects are more likely to feature in children's books than Black or Brown faces!

Winsome is passionate about changing this narrative and began fundraising on her birthday weekend of October 2019, for £50,000 to help raise awareness and educate others about the importance of having equal visual representation for multicultural children, from diverse heritage.

Areas of Expertise:
- Digital print publishing
- Content interior management
- Book layout and structure
- Copy and developmental editing
- Proofreading
- Kindle direct publishing (Digital publishing)
- Copyright
- Amazon global distribution
- Typesetting
- Marketing
- Research
- Print on demand
- Coaching
- Launch advice
- Book jacket consultation
- Copyright advice
- Six-month marketing strategy

Amazon Central Book Profile
Winsome provides creative writing online courses and workshops for budding writers. As well as her prestigious JUST WRITE IT MASTERCLASSES, at the Millennium Gloucester Hotel in Kensington and Chelsea, London. Winsome Duncan Amazon Central Book Profile: https://www.amazon.co.uk/Winsome-Duncan/e/B0034Q93UU/ref=dp_byline_cont_book_o ne

For more information about publishing your book, visit: www.peachespublications.co.uk

For children's storytelling workshops, click here: www.looklikeme.co.uk

For Book Confidence Coaching: www.bookconfidencecoach.com

Social Media:
Instagram: https://www.instagram.com/peachespublications/

Facebook: https://www.facebook.com/peachespublications/

Twitter: https://twitter.com/lyricalhealeruk

LinkedIn: https://www.linkedin.com/in/winsome-duncan-book-confidence-coach-eightfoursixtwotwoonethree7/

Marcia Brissett-Bailey Biography

Marcia Brissett-Bailey, Author, featured in Forbes, Consultant, Inspirational Speaker, Storyteller, Visual Content creator, Information Scientist, Special Education Needs and Disability (SEND) specialist and Career Advisor. Marcia has an entrepreneurial mindset, which she believes is a gift from her Dyslexia, enabling her to see her ideas in pictures and think outside the box.

She is also an advocate and champion of Dyslexia and neurodiversity. Invited as a guest speaker on various social media platforms and organisational events, she shares her experiences and personal lived journey of Dyslexia.

A co-founder of the British Dyslexia Cultural Perspective Committee, trustee at Waltham Forest Dyslexia Association, Marcia hopes to enable others with dyslexia/neurodiversity to find their voice, especially from a cultural perspective.

Marcia is a blooming author, with a passion for creative writing and performing arts. As a qualified Career Advisor, she has a particular focus on personal development, including helping young people to achieve their full potential and aspirations, by setting personal goals.

As a parent of two children, Marcia and her husband, who is an entrepreneur and property investor, are keen for their children to have opportunities in order to find their passion and purpose within business and become entrepreneurial themselves in their chosen paths in life.

Marcia has achieved a BSc in Information Science, postgraduate qualification in Career Guidance, Certificate in Person-centred Counselling Skills, a Diploma in Specialist Teaching and an MA in Special Educational Needs. She has worked in the Education Community Sector for the last 30 years and has provided information, advice and guidance in Higher Education and post-16 education settings, as well as being a SEND lead.

Marcia is keen to empower others to find their voice, working from a place of acceptance and self-love, which Marcia has had to work on to achieve, as she was always told what she cannot, instead of what she can. Marcia's chapter in this book is about creating opportunities, feeling the fear and doing it anyway, as well as sharing her entrepreneurial mindset, which includes taking opportunities and running with them, learning to say no and going with her inner voice and gut feeling and saying that's ok.

https://www.instagram.com/theblackdyslexic/

http://linkedin.com/in/marcia-brissett-bailey-bsc-pg-dip-qcg-ma-ipsea-6315a2b8

Melanie Folkes-Mayers Biography

Melanie is an award-winning HR specialist, with over 15 years' Strategic and Operational Human resource experience, across a range of industries including Retail, IT, Healthcare, Education and Local Government. The author of *Leading for Growth*, Melanie is particularly passionate about developing proactive leaders and managers, who support their teams to take ownership and deliver excellence.

Melanie loves working with Entrepreneurs and CEOs, helping them to grow and scale their operations, by providing bespoke HR Support and Advice. In 2014, she created 'Eden Mayers HR Consulting' to help her clients to deliver their passion, knowing that their People Management is in safe hands, or as Melanie calls it, "Keeping Them Out of HR Trouble".

When Melanie isn't busy supporting her clients, she's up early running, jumping out of planes and keeping up with her adventurous 5 and 7-year-old daughters.

www.edenmayers.com,
www.instagram.com/edenmayershr,
info@edenmayers.com

Shona Kamau Biography

Shona Kamau is a London-based Christian Life Coach, creating coaching programmes for women, with her personal development book soon to be released, (*Loving Yourself God's Way)*. Shona's life experiences and having gone through healing in many areas of her life, allow her to support to women who have gone through different types of trauma, from hair loss, physical, sexual and emotional abuse. Via VLG Coaching, Shona's work entails giving women the tools to heal, find love and self-acceptance after emotional trauma. I help my clients build healthy relationships with themselves and through a Christian lens. The women I work with are able to transform their lives through my one-to-one coaching, workshops and speaking engagements.

Shona is a student at London Southbank University, in her final year of her accounting and finance degree.

Shona lives and studies at her home in London, with her husband and four beautiful children and spends her time reading and listening to audiobooks, dedicated to spending time and building a continuous intimate relationship with God and maintaining a continuously joyful relationship with her children and husband.

Email: virtuouslivingbygrace@gmail.com
Website: www.virtuouslivingbygrace.com
Instagram: www.instagram.com/vlg_coaching

Joanna Oliver Biography

Joanna Oliver is a mum of three, passionately committed to helping people to grow and flourish in their personal/professional life.

Having left school aged fifteen, Joanna went on to obtain a 2:1 BA (hons) Advertising, Media and Marketing, an MA in Therapeutic Child Care and an MA in Education. Currently, Joanna teaches on a BA (hons) programme in Counselling, Coaching and Mentoring and foundation studies in Education and holds professional qualifications in Vocational Assessment, Supervision and Further Education teaching, alongside certificates in coaching and leadership.

Joanna's experience includes working with care leavers and providing group supervision for a team of local authority social workers, writing and delivering a Parent Support Programme and personal development workshops/counselling qualification with adults with physical and/or mental health challenges and returners to work. Joanna worked for a number of years for a charity in Westminster, writing and delivering volunteer induction training, facilitating group supervision, management committee 'away days' and undertaking family assessments.

Alongside teaching at University, Joanna has delivered professional training and undertaken therapeutic and functional group work with others. Her academic career led to her speaking at conferences in European universities, including Milan, Padua, Thessaloniki and Seville and in the UK.

Joanna currently provides bid writing, training, mentoring and strategic guidance for organisations and leaders, including a semi-independence accommodation for young people, an organisation working with young women who have been exploited and numerous charities working with young people, especially those most at risk. A recent development is the 'Bids n Pieces' podcast, to be found on Spotify. Additionally, Joanna has undertaken various ghost-writing, proof reading and editing projects, including e-books, blogs, court reports, press releases, web copy and chapter books. Joanna is the proud proof-reader for this Anthology.

Via ConsultaChameleon, Joanna has developed a range of on and off-line programmes, including 'Grow Free From Shackles', 'Grow Your Colours' and a set of navigational and affirmational Clarity Cards and advocates living in an aligned, intuitive and congruent way.

www.consultachameleon.co.uk
www.consultachameleon.com
https://www.linkedin.com/in/consultachameleon
https://www.instagram.com/consultachamelon

Ruth Pearson Biography

Ruth Pearson is the founder of 'Listening to Your Voice Ltd' and 'Listening to Your Voice Publishing'. She is also a secondary school Teacher, with over thirty years' experience working in a range of London schools, ranging from those deemed 'outstanding' to those requiring 'special measures'. Following the completion of her National Professional Qualification for Headship (NPQH) and whilst studying for her MA in Education, researching ways to improve teaching and learning using coaching skills, she became the sole Deputy Headteacher in her school. This role allowed her to develop a wide range of leadership skills. During a career break and to compliment her educational skills, she trained as an Accredited Master Coach, specialising in the areas of Conflict Resolution and Mediation and Wellbeing, as a Corporate Mental Health Facilitator.

Her area of unique expertise is the development of her own coaching and training model, 'Empowering Transformations'. This model puts the individual, and the choices they make, at the heart of personal development. They also learn how they can overcome challenges in life, by using them as stepping-stones to greater opportunities. This model looks at seven areas of wellbeing and how they are interlinked with each other.

Empowering Transformations, also coaches teams to work collaboratively and learn from each other, with everyone using their own unique gifts and skills. This is one of the main reasons Ruth is passionate about supporting leaders, so they can be motivated to learn, in both their personal and professional lives, as learning is a lifelong process.

Ruth is the author/co-author of eight books. Her self-help coaching book, *'Say Yes To New Opportunities! Be Motivated to L.E.A.R.N.',* integrates her expertise in the areas of motivation, wellbeing and leadership. Her publishing company specialises in the area of faith-based books, education and wellbeing.

Email: info@ltyvpublishing.co.uk
ruth.pearson@listeningtoyourvoice.co.uk
https://www.linkedin.com/in/ruthpearsonltyv/

Anna B Sexton Biography

Anna is an artist, social entrepreneur and curator of Creative Educational Content that inspires creativity and nurtures talent in people across diverse communities, globally. She has over 30 years' experience, working within the arts, creative industries, education, digital, regeneration and social care sectors. She founded 'Open To Create…' as a social enterprise, using open, collaborative and creative thinking-led approaches to come up with creative responses to pressing issues in communities, such as, lived experience of mental health; seen and unseen disabilities and access to digital skills.

Clients include: The V&A, UCL, UAL, G Adventures, Google, The Princes Trust, Mental Health Foundation, Conway Hall, Dulwich Picture Gallery, Diabetes UK, You Make It, Hackney Museum, London Transport Museum, London South Bank University, LSE. She uses a range of creative thinking, making, coaching, enterprise mentoring and person-centred facilitation skills, to co-create bespoke confidence building, professional development and business development training courses.

These courses open learners up to their unique skills and talents with the aim that they can take their new motivation into enhancing any areas of their lives. Skilled at sales, fundraising and business development, Anna has been involved in raising over

£10 million worth of investment, via money and in-kind/pro bono services over the last 15 years. She has co-founded a series of peer-to-peer development networks for creatives and start up business owners, such as We Love Marlborough and East London Creative Business Women's Network. She is a member of Antiuniversity NOW and The Other MA (TOMA); peer-led alternative education communities finding new, sustainable and self-directed ways to sharing ideas, creative skills and opportunities. Her motto is, "You do not have to be an artist to be creative" and her passion is supporting anyone she meets to discover their own creative 'thing' that lights them up.

https://www.linkedin.com/in/open-to-create-anna-b-sexton/
www.annabsexton.com
www.opentocreate.com

Patricia Bidi Biography

Studio Bidi is an art business and Patricia Bidi is its Creative Director. She is a visual artist, with a BA in Animation, working in painting and printmaking. Her art exhibit is focussed upon visions of life-affirming energy and as a result, people feel inspired, playful and joyful. Her art exhibitions and events create stimulating and engaging experiences that awaken the senses, memory and curiosity. It also encourages the active participation of the imagination with a sense of wonder and a profound appreciation for life. Her mission is to take people on a journey of creativity and transformation.

Bidi's linocut prints celebrate life's seminal moments and new beginnings, through her playful and poetic imagination, perpetually submerging the viewer within her own dynamic iconography, her own realm of storytelling. Each print is a meaningful reflection and a unique celebration of life, that touches people's hearts.

Her work has been featured in "ES Magazine" as "Sweet Dreams, exploring her Peruvian background alongside the experience of living in London. Patricia Bidi's latest exhibition, 'Dreams & Traces' transforms the Westminster Reference Library into a carnival of colour, with her vibrant linocuts", August 2019

Her linocut workshops are part of Vo Curations Contemporary Gallery Cultural Programme. These workshops bring people together to embrace, learn and engage with their creativity, cultivating a sense of community and collaboration, whilst experimenting with new ideas, materials and techniques.

Bidi led The ReadFest: Illustration and Visual Illustration 2020-2021 Workshops, at Pen to Print from Barking & Dagenham Libraries. She is an artist member of Art Can, in 2021 the collective exhibitions she is participating in are Self-Identify, Momentum, and Prelude. These events and group exhibitions show the creative spirit of London, displaying strength, perseverance, and resilience.

https://patriciabidi.com
https://patriciabidi.artelista.com/en/
https://www.instagram.com/patriciabidi
https://www.linkedin.com/in/patriciabidi/https://www.artrabbit.com/people/patriciabidi/artist

Linnette James Biography

With a vivid imagination and the ability to put words together that can captivate the mind, combined with a passion for helping, transforming and making a difference in the lives of others, it has been my childhood dream to become an author, poet and a nurse. In 2004, I was able to successfully complete a BSc (hons) in Mental Health Nursing and embarked on my nursing career within the NHS. My first piece of work was published in 1996, after entering an American based competition - "The National Library of Poetry", with one of my poems.

I have also written and published three books of my own, one of which is fictional and the other two depicting my life stories. I have been quite privileged in being able to contribute to academic books within the field of Mental Health Nursing, which have been utilized by nursing students, tutors and peers. My greatest ambition and living passion, is to be able to help, encourage and promote the self-esteem and self-belief of others. I'm currently studying a BA in Theology, with the hopes that this will aid my literary approach, in being more holistic.

www.linkedin.com/in/linnette-james-84ba7596

https://www.instagram.com/linnettejamessow/

Useful Links

Genius within
https://www.geniuswithin.co.uk/

British Dyslexia Association
https://www.bdadyslexia.org.uk/

Access to Work Scheme
https://www.gov.uk/access-to-work

Atwoi Dyslexia
https://www.atwoidyslexia.com/

Exceptional individuals
https://exceptionalindividuals.com/

Do-It Solutions
https://doitprofiler.com/discover-do-it/about-us/

Antiuniversity Now
http://antiuniversity.org/

More to Life training programmes
https://moretolife.org/

The Artist Way by Julia Cameron
https://juliacameronlive.com/

Personal Values
https://personalvalu.es/

Mind
https://www.mind.org.uk/

Mind Tools
https://www.mindtools.com/

Young Minds
https://youngminds.org.uk/

ACAS
https://www.acas.org.uk/

MHFA England
https://mhfaengland.org/

Federation of Small Business (FSB)
https://www.fsb.org.uk/

Reflective Notes

Reflective Notes

Reflective Notes

Reflective Notes

Reflective Notes

Reflective Notes

Reflective Notes

Reflective Notes

Reflective Notes

Reflective Notes

Reflective Notes

Printed in Great Britain
by Amazon